# SOFTWARE Rx
## Secrets of Engineering Quality Software

Rodney C. Wilson

To join a Prentice Hall PTR
internet mailing list, point to
http://www.prenhall.com/register

**PRENTICE HALL PTR**
Upper Saddle River, New Jersey 07458
http://www.prenhall.com

**Library of Congress Cataloging-in-Publication Data**
Wilson, Rodney C.
    Software Rx: secrets of engineering quality software/Rodney C.
Wilson.
        p.   cm.
    Includes bibliographical references and index.
    ISBN 0-13-472663-4
    1. Software engineering.  2. Computer software—Quality control.
I. Title
QA76.758.W54   1997
005.1—dc20

96-27619
CIP

Acquisitions Editor: *Michael Meehan*
Production Editor: *Kerry Reardon*
Copy Editor: *Henry Pels*
Cover Design: *Wanda Espána*
Manufacturing Manager: *Alexis R. Heydt*
Cover Design Director: *Jerry Votta*

©1997 Prentice Hall PTR
Prentice-Hall, Inc.
A Simon & Schuster Company
Upper Saddle River, New Jersey 07458

This book was composed in FrameMaker.

The publisher offers discounts on this book
when ordered in bulk quantities.
For more information contact:

Corporate Sales Department
Pentice Hall PTR
One Lake Street
Upper Saddle River, N.J. 07458
Phone: 800-382-3419 / FAX: 201-236-7141
E-mail: corpsales@prenhall.com

Printed in the United States of America

10   9   8   7   6   5   4   3   2   1

ISBN  0-13-472663-4

Prentice-Hall International (UK) Limited, *London*
Prentice-Hall of Australia Pty. Limited, *Sydney*
Prentice-Hall Canada Inc., *Toronto*
Prentice-Hall Hispanoamericana, S.A., *Mexico*
Prentice-Hall of India Private Limited, *New Delhi*
Prentice-Hall of Japan, *Tokyo*
Simon & Schuster Asia Pte. Ltd., *Singapore*
Editora Prentice-Hall do Brasil, Ltda., *Rio de Janeiro*

*To my wife and my parents.*

# Contents

Chapter 4 The Phased Approach 39

# Chapter 9 Assertions (Making Your Source Code Robust) 109

# Chapter 10 Best Practices for Software Testing 119

# Preface

This book contains a collection of best practices for software engineers, developers, testers, and project and program managers. Software engineering is an extremely broad subject and best practices are open to very broad interpretation. In fact, there are many alternative approaches to best practices. Therefore this book is a collection of a personal software processes used throughout the development life cycle by lead engineers of some of the largest software engineering organizations in the world. Many more formal approaches are available than those provided by this text. The author's intent, however, is to showcase the practical application of many formal software engineering methods. Validation of each claim is provided by the fact that most practices were perceived as "best" in the organization using quality measurement criteria such as return on investment, customer orientation, and sustained improvement over time. These practices were also selected by the author based on his experience in the field of software engineering for the last sixteen years.

Several essays and suggestions for software development and test engineering practitioners are provided based on real-life project team experiences. Again, software engineering is an extremely broad subject, therefore, references are provided throughout to point the reader to more detailed information on a specific topic.

This text is composed of a number of chapters that deal with everything from source code assertions to engineering discipline and rigor. Examples are used throughout to give readers an understanding of modern-day best practices associated with the development, testing, and release of software workproducts.

# Software Engineering Best Practices

Competitive software development and delivery methods, tools, and processes are critical ingredients for releasing successful software products. The requirement for software engineering best practices applies to both application and system software companies.

Just understanding the development tools (e.g., C, C++, **dbx**, **lint**) is not enough to ensure project and product success. Understanding software engineering principles such as task analysis, assertions, configuration management, paper prototypes, design and code reviews, and other best practices is equally important to tool knowledge.

The author's intent is that this book be used as a handbook by project team leaders and individual contributors. After all, these are the individuals challenged with delivering high-quality software products to customers and users according to aggressive market-driven schedules.

If you are looking for a book to provide practical and industry-proven methods of delivering production-quality software to your customers, you will find this book a useful and welcome addition to your library.

This book is based on real-life (practical) methods and processes for developing and delivering software products. This book answers the common question of: "How can I improve the quality of my products prior to customer delivery?" Several best practices associated with software engineering process rigor are discussed, for example, using assertions to reduce source code failures and the risk associated with inadequately tested and reviewed software programs.

## Contents

Key benefits and rewards associated with design and code reviews are discussed in detail. Also, potential problems resulting from not performing design reviews are explored to help pilot the process of reviews in your organization. How to change company cultures from viewing detailed designs and documentation as a burden to an important requirement for success is also discussed. The following additional best practices are included:

- The need for teamwork and team development as critical core competencies for success. Teamwork among cross-functional project teams (individuals from multiple disciplines) is key to the successful release of software products. Most modern-day software development projects require the effort of many dedicated individuals working in various areas of expertise. These project team members must move in the same direction for project and ultimately product success. Many key attributes of a successful team are discussed.

- The *big bang approach* does not work for software integration, as many have learned. The same is true for software development. Instead, a phased approach is required during the software development process to ensure successful release of modern-day software programs.

- Reviews and inspections are still infrequently performed successfully, even though these software quality methods are not new to the development process. Several tips and traps associated with the review process are included in this text to help the reader. Reviews are critical to product and company success. They are something every project team member must understand.

- Key issues surrounding design specifications are also discussed, and why most developers and project team members hate to develop these vital documents.

- Object-oriented programming, analysis, design, and implementation do not reduce the need for a software engineering methodology, they increase it! This chapter discusses how to increase and leverage the value of object-oriented methods to their fullest extent.

- How to successfully use prototypes, specifications, and reviews. This chapter contains a collection of best practices for the development of GUI and non-GUI-based software applications.

- The benefit and use of source code assertions. How to increase testability and reliability by wisely using assertions in production-level source code.

- Vital success metrics are used for unit, integration, system, and acceptance testing. These metrics ensure that what is delivered meets the customer's acceptance criteria. In other words, how to avoid surprises after the product is released to the customer.

- Survey results from a verification and validation best-in-breed interview with a successful software development company is also included. This chapter discusses the cultural and individual characteristics of a mature software development organization.

- The Ambiguity Reviews Appendix is a must for anyone reviewing any type of document (e.g., everything from legal agreements to functional specifications). This appendix includes a collection of approximately twelve items provided courtesy of Richard Bender of Bender & Associates.

This section of the book covers issues such as the dangling *else* condition, "i.e.," vs. "e.g.," temporal, functional, reference, and omission ambiguities.

# Audience

This book is recommended as a supplement to both introductory and intermediate software engineering courses conducted at local universities. Seasoned computer professionals also benefit from the practical suggestions provided in this text. The industrial sector served includes software engineering managers and project leaders. Other audiences include anyone who wants to cultivate a software development process which reflects current industry best practices.

Another target audience includes all new software engineering project leaders. Oftentimes, these individuals have a proven technical track record; however, they are now breaking new ground as project team leaders. New skills, such as team building, cross-functional team communication, and design and code reviews are some of the many project leader requirements discussed in this text.

Welcome to *Software Rx: Secrets of Engineering Quality Software*. I hope you find this book a valuable collection of modules for project, product, and ultimately company success.

Several individuals are responsible for helping to review this text. I would like to thank the following individuals for their help: Keith Stobie (Informix Software), Maxine Crother (Cadence Design Systems), Akira Fujimura (Pure Software), Ray Kehoe (Intel Corporation), Dr. Larry Wear (Wear Consulting), Doug Hoffman (Software Quality Methods), Greg Daich (Software Technology Support Center), Dr. Roger Pressman (RGPA), Naresh Bala (Mercury Interactive Corporation), and Andrew Ferlitsch (Quality Engineering Technologies, Inc.).

I would especially like to thank many of the developers at Cadence Design Systems for their input, which provided the basis and foundation for this book. Also, for her valuable contribution, research, and review of this book, I would like to thank Belinda Juran, one of the key contributors for cultivating and documenting best practices at Cadence. I would also like to thank my wife and parents for their encouragement in completing this difficult project.

# Biography

Rodney C. Wilson is the Quality Architect for Cadence Design Systems and author of *UNIX Test Tools and Benchmarks*, and *UNIX Tamed*, Prentice Hall (1995). He has developed, managed, and tested computer hardware and software (applications, networking, operating systems and languages), since 1979. His accomplishments include the successful release of UNIX BSD and SVR4, MACH, DOS, and MS Windows products. Computer systems include a notebook to moderately parallel supercomputers. Mr. Wilson has conducted several seminars as an instructor with the UC extension for over four years. Courses conducted include:

- Design, Develop and Execute Functional and System Test Cases
- Introduction to UNIX System V Release 4
- UNIX System V Release 4 Administration I and II
- UNIX Standards and Benchmarks
- UNIX Security for System Administrators
- PERL Programming

# Software Engineering
# Best Practices

# 1

**H**ow do you achieve high customer satisfaction? Through a blend of cross-functional team communication, technical and people-skill knowledge, and a win-win attitude you can delight your customers. In this chapter, we identify several software engineering best practices, however, attitude makes the difference between success and failure. Attitude is the key to cultivating and maintaining software engineering best practices. As Charles Swindoll said, "I am convinced that life is 10 percent what happens to me and 90 percent how I react to it."

## 1.1 Vocabulary (keywords)

awards, Capability Maturity Matrix (CMM), checklists, fire fighting, customer satisfaction, errors, failures, faults, functional specification, functional testing, guidelines, hacking, impact analysis, ISO9000, metrics, minimal unit test case determination, pride of ownership, Quality Assurance (QA), quality awards, quality engineering, Quality Functional Deployment (QFD), regressions, reflective questions, reliability engineering, requirements specification, root cause analysis, Software Engineering Institute (SEI), software failures, standards, structural testing, testability, testware, usability

## 1.2 Awards and Attitude

Many companies use division and corporate quality awards to reward best practices for software engineering excellence. Most software companies have learned that fire fighting and hacking may provide short-term results, however, in the long run they are deadly. Fire fighting only results in high employee turnover (low morale), customer dissatisfaction, and poor company financial results.

The Chief Executive Officer (CEO), or another executive staff member, presents an award to the project team for cultivating and sustaining best practices. (Hopefully, they understand and can explain why they are presenting the award, if not, this is just an empty formality.) This plaque is usually accompanied by a check for each individual. Quality and special achievement awards are provided to teams for various accomplishments (e.g., reducing the total number of outstanding customer problem reports or practicing software development process rigor—design and code reviews). An award or special achievement is usually the result of adopting new tools and processes which result in increased customer satisfaction.

This book is about exploring and using methods and tools (best practices) which result in the receipt of a quality award. The objective is for you and your team to win an award, either internal or external. Many companies challenge their managers with ISO9000 certification [ISO91]. They also challenge them with increasing the organization's maturity level based on the Software Engineering Institute's (SEI) Capability Maturity Matrix (CMM) [CROS79]. In fact, many bonus checks are now dependent on reaching the next level of maturity, not just release of the product according to schedule.

If a plaque is provided along with the award, it is important to identify the project team and not a single individual. Acknowledging the team is important, since individuals may leave the company for various reasons (e.g., down-sizing, right-sizing, and even termination). When an individual leaves the company (at their request or the company's), the quality award plaque's value continues long after individual team members have left. The team's excellence should always be noted, not any single individual's performance when a quality or special achievement award is presented. Another important reason for using this approach is to accent that teamwork is valued by the organization. (The enemy is the competition, never your project team member or co-worker.)

Successful software companies are careful when rewarding a team with any type of quality award (e.g., division, group, or corporate). In some cases, the team is disinterested in pursuing new approaches and methods to software development, since no new goals have been identified, or are even required for success. Inflated egos are always counterproductive to teamwork and team development and growth. On the other hand, some teams—such as The Black Team—were famous for their zeal in finding defects [DEMA87].

Executive management must not only focus on customer complaint reduction, problem reports, or time to release, but overall measurable and continuous quality improvement. Success is truly achieved when process and product improvements are sustained throughout the entire software development life cycle. This is an important criteria for evaluating each quality award nomination. After all, there is much more to customer satisfaction than repairing problems. The majority of all software customers prefer problem avoidance (prevention), to problem detection and repair.

Always seek to design and develop products throughout the entire development process with the customer in mind, not just at the end (e.g., during the beta test phase). Never simply sit back and wait for repairs (rework) after shipment. The software industry has grown too accustomed to simply sending patches to the field, rather than striving for customer satisfaction and zero defects. Zero defects is one of many motivations for cultivating and propagating best practices (a passion of the author and primary motivation for this book). Furthermore, these practices must apply (be tailored) to both mission-critical as well as rapid-delivery feature-rich environments [IEEE_SOFTWARE].

## 1.3 Ingredients For Best Practices

Some of many factors which are important ingredients, or best practices, for software development include:

- Definition, adoption, and maintenance of a rigorous software development process from product concept to end of life (phase containment).
- Definition, collection, analysis, and action associated with process, code, and test metrics [GRAD92].
- Successful communication between cross-functional team members (i.e., employees working well with other individuals from different disciplines).
- Timely response to problems (e.g., discovery, follow-up, and closure).
- Quality engineering (testing and analysis using metrics, standards, and automated tools) [WILS95]. Quality engineering also includes fault recovery (trap handlers and test assertions), defensive design, and requirements, design, and source code modularity.
- Code maintainability using standards and guidelines.
- Usability engineering (task analysis and usability testing) [PRES92].
- Reliability engineering (testing and analysis based on use-models and operational profiles). For example, if 30 percent of overall system usage is expected to come from function x, 30 percent of all reliability testing includes this function.

- Functional testing, definition, design, and development (e.g., mapping requirements to designs and source code).
- Structural testing (e.g., static and dynamic source code analysis).

## 1.4 Pride Of Ownership

All of the preceding practices are sustained over a significant period prior to team nomination and receipt of a quality award. Pride of ownership (attitude) is an underlying and vital attribute associated with all software engineering best practices. Software product owners must ensure that their functions, libraries, and routines are properly maintained. A complete chapter on teamwork is provided later in this book.

There is no difference between a software engineering workproduct and real-estate, or property ownership. Both software and property either appreciate or depreciate depending on the amount of pride of ownership applied. Each engineer must feel that they own the workproduct, at least their portion of a module, or function. My research shows that when developers can no longer include their name in product source code, code quality suffers significantly. Asking developers to take responsibility without accountability is impractical. Make sure to include a means to ensure accountability along with responsibility for the following release deliverables, not just the source code:

- Functional requirements specification [PRES92]
- Preliminary and detailed design specifications [PRES92]
- Architecture document and all relevant functional interfaces
- All source code (e.g., header files, source code, build files, and libraries)
- Test plans, test matrices (for test design), and incident reports [WILS95]
- Testware (e.g., golden data files, tests, drivers, and documentation)

Ownership is the key ingredient to driving corporate culture change and developing best practices for software development, however, documenting disciplined processes, which are promoted as best practices, is equally critical. Documenting processes allows team members to develop and to maintain high-quality products.

Without well-documented checklists, guidelines, or standards, best practices usually leave when an individual takes a new assignment, or leaves the company. Metrics are another best practice to measure success and build accountability into the project team culture.

Loyalty and longevity are key ingredients to quality, however, engineers are expected to change assignments frequently. In the Silicon Valley during the 1980s, many software engineers would change companies and assignments every two years. Engineers today still change job responsibilities frequently, however, larger companies use job rotation to keep their key contributors from leaving the organization.

## 1.5  Job Rotation and Sharing Information

Job rotation is one of the best methods for propagating best practices. Unfortunately, this practice is seldom used by many software organizations. This is a shame, since both the customer and the vendor will lose. Provide the transition to job rotation by inviting other project and product team members (e.g., Quality Assurance (QA), technical support, and technical publications) to development and other functional staff meetings. Never take the attitude of: "I only invite QA engineers when the team is going to discuss quality issues." If you have project team members who are interested in growing and learning (e.g., product source code, design, architecture), invite them to your staff meetings. Attending staff meetings is more informal than job rotation, however, it still provides good cross-functional communication between project team members.

Individuals from QA, technical publications, and customer support are potentially excellent replacements for junior or lead developers. After all, quality consciousness and the ability to document and to communicate clearly are key attributes for successful software developers and project team members. Also, how about developers trying out QA, technical publications, and customer support? Cranking out code quickly does not mean that a developer has all the skills required for delighting customers with new products and features. Job rotation also includes having developers work in the support center, QA, training, technical support, and other project team functions. In other words, hold open staff meetings by allowing other project team members the opportunity to learn and participate in all aspects of product development and allow them the opportunity to make the transition to new roles.

## 1.6  Customer Interaction

Successful project teams are in constant communication and correspondence with select (key) customers. Have your developers, writers, program managers, and testers listen to their customers (both internal and external) on a frequent basis. You can learn much from the customer when you listen carefully (more about methods and techniques for this practice shortly). By better understanding your customer's needs, you can save hours, days, weeks, and even months of effort further down the road (i.e., you shorten the overall development cycle). The overall process may seem slower at first, however, significant increases are realized (expected) at each successful milestone.

The product marketing engineer or manager must share the responsibility for collecting, analyzing, and documenting customer requirements, however, the technical or product marketing individual is required to act as the central point for customer contact. Engineers frequently interact with marketing in order to understand customer requirements. Many companies require marketing to create a concept proposal to direct and provide guidance to the requirements document. Engineering must create a functional specification from the marketing concept proposal to document specific features for implementing. Both documents are always carefully reviewed with the customer to ensure success.

When you pay special attention (listen carefully) to your customers, they will state a solution to a perceived problem, instead of a problem or failure. The customers may state their position as though they were describing a problem, however, when you listen carefully, notice that a condition or symptom of a problem is articulated. Rarely will you hear customers articulating the root cause (underlying reason for the failure).

Customers usually are angry or impatient when describing a problem. Therefore, it is very important to learn how to avoid punches. Never become defensive during a discussion with the customer. Always let the customer vent first (if necessary) before trying to diagnose the problem. Consider using tools such as, Quality Function Deployment (QFD), focus groups, and customer satisfaction surveys to improve customer communication and interaction. Having an unbiased facilitator is also a useful way to get positive results from customer-developer meetings.

Always focus your questions and discussion on the issue and not the person (lead by example). In other words, get into the practice of starting with non-defensive questions during the interview. For example:

- What specific task are you going to accomplish?
- What tools, methods, and processes (functions) are frequently used?
- Why is this the best approach to use?

Always identify priorities when more than a single issue is at hand. Categorizing problems by must, should, or could is one method. It is always important to attempt to separate wants from needs, especially when other customer requirements are impending. Most customers have a preconceived notion of the desired product behavior. Therefore, what is expressed (verbally or otherwise) does not reflect the true underlying need (requirement and solution).

One example of poor customer communication is when an additional function is desired but already exists in the current product. Another common problem is when a new function is implemented (without review). This condition results in product usability and testability problems, since unnecessary complexity (redundancy) is introduced.

Project team members must know how to discern true needs from perceived or believed desires. This discernment is obtained through rephrasing the problem in the form of a reflective question. For example, "So let me see if I really understand, what you are saying is... " Providing a solution to a problem that does not exist does not engender a satisfied customer, it may even make the situation worse.

Always strive to provide a complete solution which solves the overall problem, not an immediate symptom or perceived need. This can only occur if you start by identifying the true underlying need. As is the case with root cause analysis, this goal requires extra effort. On the other hand, solving the problem properly greatly outweighs the accounting and lost opportunity costs of providing the wrong solution (i.e., more rework and lost productivity).

Once you have identified the true underlying need, always provide only the best-fit solution for just that need and no more. Providing additional capabilities only increases product complexity and decreases usability, testability, reliability, maintainability, and performance.

## 1.7 Reflective Questions

*Reflective questions* are a simple method of communication where the listener repeats what the speaker just said (in a paraphrased sentence). One example of a statement requiring a reflective question is when someone says, "We have decided to use the existing user interface in the 4.5 release, instead of using the new one provided in 5.0." One example of a reflective question to the preceding statement is, "So you will not change the user interface in the 5.0 release?" See the appendix on ambiguity reviews for details regarding removing ambiguity in the English language.

Using reflective questions during customer (internal and external) reviews is vital to success. Remember, many engineers (humans) speak different technical, cultural, body, and human languages. Body language is very difficult to discern using the telephone or electronic mail. This is also the case with many teleconference systems that operate on a 5 frame-per-second basis. Therefore, consider increasing your sensitivity level during these meetings and discussions. Written words are especially dangerous, since they can be interpreted incorrectly. Show special care in all non-verbal communication settings. The English language is imprecise and many English words were designed to have multiple definitions.

Always communicate (especially electronically) without phrases or abstract technical terms. If you must use special or technical terms, make sure to include a glossary or dictionary of terms. (This is also a best practice for writing source code and developing design documentation). Use an index to focus the review and maintenance effort (i.e., newcomers are better able to understand the structure and layout of the source code).

Acronyms and buzzwords almost always guarantee a misunderstanding (especially between customers and software vendors). Clarify each statement to the greatest extent possible. One example of clarification is making sure to include checks for ambiguity before you submit a response. Some of the many potential checks available are included in the appendix on ambiguity reviews. This type of analysis is useful for almost any type of workproduct (e.g., requirements, design, code, and documentation).

## 1.8  Customer Satisfaction (Your Number One Priority)

Never procrastinate when it comes to supporting your customers (both internal and external). Software failures which result in work stoppage are always your number one priority (i.e., prevention, detection, containment, and resolution). Enhancement requests are usually always a number two priority, however, you must understand why these problems were not identified in the original functional requirements or design specification. High-quality code is usually always more important than extended functionality, except for special circumstances (e.g., throw-away prototypes used to model a new technology) [IEEE_SOFTWARE95].

Once you and your team eliminate the majority of problem reports, it becomes much easier to keep up with customer demand for new features and repairs. Do not allow yourself and the team to get behind the power curve (i.e., the number of incoming problems outweighs the number of fixed problems on a daily or weekly basis).

When possible, always attempt to perform root cause analysis on each problem (see the appendix on root cause analysis for details). Attempt to identify and contain the missing barriers or product changes which are the perceived contributors to each problem. What barriers (test, analysis, or review) do you believe would have prevented the problem from occurring? What changes to the work product were responsible for the failure? Perform root cause analysis on all critical issues and on other issues as time permits.

If you and your team do not remain caught up with the problem report backlog, you end up in the same situation in which most engineers seem to find themselves—always fighting fires. Make sure to strive to provide a proper balance between the following three key items for customer and company success:

- Problem report backlog
- New features and schedule
- Prevention through root cause failure analysis and process development

## 1.9   The Quality Mind-set

One important key to success is really having a strong (mature) mind-set (i.e., a team development-oriented attitude). High-quality products never just happen. Everyone on the project team must strive to continue to improve the process. In other words, everyone on the team must feel a deep sense of ownership. Successful software developers say: "This is our product and we must care for it as if it is our baby. Everyone must feel proud of the product and always want to see the customer delighted." This means that all functions provide the correct results, promptly, based on clear documentation with useful (practical) examples.

The quality mind-set evaluates if a proposed change disrupts existing modules, functions, libraries, or the overall system architecture. When the measured risk (source code or design complexity, testability, reliability, or structural integrity) is significant, a new function is required. Always strive to understand if the same function is possible using a different technical method, management process, or proven method, or if an alternative tool or product technology provides a better solution to the problem than the current method used.

Customer satisfaction is a result of a quality-oriented company culture. You must have a customer-oriented solution-oriented mind-set to successfully compete in most software and hardware markets today. The customer must always come first (e.g., above your own priorities for tasks that you would prefer to accomplish—new development). After all, the customer is the individual who pays money to purchase your product, which in turn pays your salary. If the product does not work correctly, you must feel responsible and want to go and fix the problem immediately.

On the other hand, if the customer is not using the product properly (according to the on-line or hard-copy documentation or training material), you must ensure that they are properly trained. Training is not always the answer to usability problems, as some customers do not invest in training. This type of infrastructure neglect (lack of process, training, support, and management) usually results in missed schedules, or even critical financial loss. On the other hand, developers trained in usability are never happy with simply sending a new user to a training class. A customer-oriented mind-set is based on the desire to understand the root cause of all problems (pilot errors or otherwise). Better yet, it should be based on the desire to prevent failures from occurring in the first place by avoiding errors from becoming faults and failures [IEEE94, WILS95].

## 1.10 No Quick and Dirty Fixes

Successful project leaders balance customer satisfaction with the design and development of high-quality code. This includes well-designed and well-written code which conforms to project team standards and guidelines. Source code written according to the team's, or company's standard is always easier to support and enhance than a personal style (a *hack*) no one can understand.

A hack is a quick fix to a problem that is not expected to last long, instead of a complete solution based on the team's standards for excellence. A quick and dirty fix may solve the immediate need, but rarely provides a long-term solution to the real problem. Compatibility, interoperability, or reliability failure are bound to occur from a source code hack. Developers who use a development process (with discipline and rigor) from the concept phase to first customer shipping are better able to satisfy critical customer's needs (especially in the long term). These individuals are also viewed with respect by their managers and even in some cases peers (these are the best mentor candidates in the organization). Discipline and rigor often mean simply using the word "no" to new requests.

## 1.11  Development Process Diligence

The entire discussion of software engineering as a practice is quite volatile and is debated over the Internet in *comp.software* and *comp.software.testing*. Software engineering is one of only a few professions where human lives are sometimes at risk (e.g., medical, defense and aviation) as a result of poorly trained employees. One example of this risk is when practicing software engineers are unfamiliar with the Institute of Electrical and Electronics Engineers (IEEE) software engineering standards.

All that is typically required to determine process (due) diligence is:

- Proper care was used during product development (requirements and design specifications, source code control, and testing)
- A standard was followed (when available—IEEE)
- Testing was conducted (based on a standard—minimal unit test determination and functional test coverage) [IEEE94, WILS95]
- A problem occurred and was resolved

What is interesting is that the IEEE standard for *minimal unit test determination* requires a test for each statement (instruction) in the program's source code logic. On the other hand, most software and hardware companies (approximately 80 percent) do not use any structural testing methods. These methods are used to determine how much of the source code is tested using control- or data-flow techniques. What is even more ironic is that there are many coverage analysis tools available on the market [WILS95].

*Functional test coverage* measures the number of functional tests vs. the total number of product features [WILS95]. Unfortunately, the majority of software companies never measure their structural, or functional test coverage even though they are IEEE standards. Softest from Bender & Associates and MCman from Quality Assured Software Engineering are two of many tools that measure functional test coverage.

## 1.12  Discipline and Rigor

Discipline in all aspects of the product development is important to project and product success. Do not let yourself, or the project team, get into the trap of putting any change into the code without the change request being fundamental or necessary. Always consider adding well thought-out and planned additions to a function or system. Never allow schedule pressure to force developers to start slapping or bolting-on another bell or whistle at the risk of the project.

Although features and functions are perceived as the most important attribute of the development process, proper balance with quality, schedule, and resource constraints is equally critical. Hacking in another section of code to an already overburdened (muddled) function not only reduces product reliability and maintainability, system performance suffers as well.

Carefully evaluate all new product enhancements for architectural changes which are required to properly facilitate each request. Carefully review each request when the customer may not completely understand the boundaries or capabilities of the existing system or application.

## 1.13  Hacking vs. Engineering

Never code from a question to obtain an answer (e.g., what happens when we use this data or function?). This only shows lack of process and control (customer requirements). Furthermore, never write code just to get to the solution, since you may have completely misunderstood the problem, or true underlying requirement.

A *hack* is when the program no longer processes user directives or data according to customer requirements (e.g., user and function interface breakdown). Failures from hacks are also known as regressions (loss in product functionality). I believe regressions are by-products of a hack. Hacking just provides new code with regressive functionality to the customer sooner. Why would any reasonable customer want to pay for that? On the other hand, some customers want functionality more than quality, reliability, and stability.

It is simple to come up with an algorithm or piece of code to solve an immediate need and introduce great risk to the success of the project at the same time. Instead, always back up and take a look at the overall big picture (e.g., documentation, interfaces, architecture, maintenance, performance, compatibility, and reliability). Specifically, what is the general solution you are going to provide to all customers using the product?

Never just dive in (hacking source code) and start solving the immediate simple (perceived) problem. Instead, focus on solving the generic (architectural) problem, which is highly leveraged across the entire company (i.e., all products and services). The underlying problem is usually complicated to design and requires significant changes to the architecture. Complete (long-term) solutions require much more thinking and soul searching. Once the design architecture is properly defined, completing the code is much easier and more rewarding than providing a hack. The process of providing a complete solution is also much more rewarding.

Using the preceding method, each fix now works for any data type or product function anywhere in the system or solution-flow. If this is not the case, the process along with the design has failed and both are reanalyzed (which can occur). The purpose of a well-defined process is to reduce rework, with zero defects, or customer satisfaction as the mission.

Without a well-defined development process, you and your team members must rip up the design and start all over. This is never a pleasant experience, but if the redesign is approached positively, both technical and interpersonal skills are sharpened in the process. Unnecessary redesign due to a poor development process (e.g., missing architecture or design specifications) provides the incentive to develop and document the new development process.

## 1.14 Technology for Source Code Impact Analysis

Never hack, patch, and try to release a piece of code that does not work for all required data types, elements, interfaces, and structures originally designed for the product. Whenever possible, use a source code browser to evaluate the relative impact (risk assessment) to the product and customer solution as a result of your change.

Information models are developed by many software development environment tools for simulating the source code building process. Once the information models are developed, developers and testers can determine the impact to various workproducts (i.e., tests, documentation, and designs) with each source code change. Impact analysis from information model updates are especially useful during source code maintenance. This is especially true when data structures or function prototype changes are analyzed at the local level but the global impact is unknown. Analyze risk during system testing when function call exit and return codes are changed to public Application Programming Interfaces (APIs) and commonly used data structures. The risk of changing macros contained in header files is also important to consider during source code maintenance. Source code impact analysis is useful for product partitioning, dead code analysis, source browsing, and performance engineering [PRESS92, WILS95].

## 1.15 Management Support or Threats?

Never just throw together a solution, even if you are under significant pressure to put a piece of the program into production so that you can meet a release deadline. As an example, the project team at one well-known software company told management that a product was not ready for release, however, management decided to release the product anyway (so the story is told). That well known PC software company (Ashton Tate) was purchased and no longer exists today. There is a lesson for all project team members, leaders, and managers in this tragedy. Management is swayed by schedule and feature pressures to release products that do not meet or exceed customer expectations. Only one bad release has the potential to kill a company.

Complete all the tasks associated with the development life cycle before product release; otherwise, you must reset the customer's expectations (i.e., this is an alpha, or prototype release). Adding, modifying, or creating source code is usually insufficient when it comes to satisfying customer needs (e.g., documentation, training materials, lab exercises, and demonstration programs are also required).

The design, development, and execution of unit-, function-, integration-, and system-level tests is critical for product and company success. Documentation must be updated (both the requirements specification and user documentation) throughout the life cycle as a result of testing. Many successful software companies are now realizing the value of their testware and are providing higher-quality products as a result. See the chapter on testing best practices for further details.

Having the sales and field-support people provide an occasional "thank you" can go a long way toward improving employee morale and customer satisfaction. Usually, this simple gesture does not require a significant amount of effort for success. All that is really required is basic recognition and acknowledgment of the team's contribution. Many methods for rewarding employees are available, for example, cash awards, lunches, dinners, small gifts, and business trips to nice places. Most developers with whom I have worked (including myself) always work better and are motivated by kindness and respect, never by fear and intimidation (in the long term).

## 1.16 Planning is the Key

Accurate and realistic planning is another best practice that many engineering managers strive to achieve. In order to accomplish this goal, project planning, management, and estimation tools are used [WILS95]. Discipline and the use of tools (supported by empirical data) ensures that you and your project team never commit to more work than is possible. In other words, you are able to know when to say no. Credibility means using common sense to never make promises you simply cannot keep.

Always set customer expectations properly (i.e., scheduled estimates are based on a detailed statement-of-work, which includes the development and execution of acceptance tests). If you have the optimism to believe you can deliver a perfect ten, set the customer's expectations to a five (or lower depending on the history of previous customer engagements). Always ensure that each product release is better than the last (as measured by the results of process, code, and test metrics). Do not try to reach for the sky and hit a home run with each release, but continue to strive for improvement.

Contingency planning is also important to success. Everything does not always work right the first time (especially during the full integration or system test cycle). After you have made contingency plans, you never have to panic toward the end of the release—you always have a fall-back plan.

Never get stuck in a constant state of panic (normal operating procedure for most software companies). There is much more to software engineering than writing a few lines of code and getting it through the compiler successfully. You must always create your schedules with the notion of mass-market distribution (i.e., commodity distribution, shrink-wrap market competition, and market-driven development). User documentation, tests, functional specifications, detailed design documentation, and architecture specifications are also critical workproducts in addition to source code. Compliment your developers when you see them plan and implement documentation, testing, and reviews.

## 1.17 Conclusions

- Attitude is the key to successful product development and deployment.

- A project team armed with the best equipment, skilled individuals, finances, and management support is only successful when they function as a team.

- Product and company success require especially talented project leadership, along with management support (i.e., training, processes, methods, and tools). People, technology, training, and process (infrastructure) as an ensemble, not as individual items, are critical to success.

- Hold open staff meetings by allowing other project team members the opportunity to learn and participate in all aspects of product development. Using this method, you are better able to ensure successful job sharing and rotation through open communication.

- Have developers work in the customer support center and visit customers as part of a job training and rotation plan (make this voluntary and provide a benefit to participants).

- Create a new employee training class to cultivate and enhance best practices for software development (e.g., configuration management, coding standards, testing, and reviews).

- Successful project teams interact with their internal and external customers on a frequent basis. These teams also ensure that all problems have follow-up and closure.

- Attitude makes the difference. Attitude is the key to unlocking and cultivating best practices!

## 1.18 Questions

1. Why should you prepare special achievement and quality awards as a team?

2. What product deliverables, other than source code, are important to product and project success?

3. Explain the purpose of functional test coverage.

4. What is the definition of a hack? Why is this approach so dangerous?

5. Why is electronic communication (e-mail) not always the best solution to a problem?

6. What are other benefits of impact analysis?

7. What type of structural testing technique is used for the IEEE minimal unit test case determination metric?

8. What is an example of a reflective question? When is it appropriate to use this communication technique?

9. What are two important techniques used to determine the root cause of a failure?

10. What is one informal technique for sharing information between team members, other than formal job rotation?

# Teamwork

# 2

**P**rojects can face many challenges, constantly changing requirements, tight project schedules, development sites around the globe, and many other technical and interpersonal complexities. Through teamwork, dedication, and a strong passion for excellence (world-class quality), project and product success is obtained.

Success is measured as only putting out products which delight each customer and end user. Successful project teams always learn, grow, and improve from each and every project. These teams always seek to apply innovative methods and tools to the next project to improve the team's performance (and that of each team member). This chapter contains several practices for teamwork, a key ingredient for project and product success.

## 2.1 Vocabulary (keywords)

beta testing, code reviews, communication, complexity, consensus, context-sensitive help, customer use-model, design specification, distributed software development, documentation, functionality, independence, infrastructure, interdependence, marketing plan, peer reviews, product requirements, prototypes, redesign, scaleability, solutions, state transitions, synergy, task analysis, technical marketing, test stubs, training material, usability, usability testing, use-model, walkthroughs, workproducts

## 2.2 Global Localization and The Project Team

One of the biggest challenges most software project teams face is remote coordination and communication between individuals located throughout the world. Many companies are still striving to achieve success as a globally distributed development organization.

U.S. project teams may complain that their offshore counterparts are: "A black hole—send a query and it disappears." Best practice project teams are truly successful when no individual on the team expresses these types of complaints (regardless of their geographic location). The key to teamwork is moving each individual from independence to interdependence [COVE89].

Functional project teams consistently query both sides for status and expect a response within 24 hours. This type of close communication is vital to success and is required to keep all team members synchronized and on track according to the project schedule.

There are severe architectural constraints as a result of attempting to implement a new sophisticated function, especially when the effort spans the globe. Distributed software development makes consensus between individual contributors more difficult than it is when members are located in the same building, especially when you must make a difficult decision with an international cross-functional team. Successful communication requires getting all the people who have an opinion in the same room (or on the plane) with a just-do-it approach. Successful project leaders will solicit ideas from each individual and streamline the feedback into the smallest set of proposals possible. Once you have everyone assembled, the project leader selects one proposal (with the team).

Successful project teams never accept, or simply say: "We do not like the proposal", without providing an alternate suggestion or solution. These project teams are also comprised of individuals who always have, or strive for solutions (a can-do attitude). Not all solutions require a technical approach. Oftentimes the best solution requires a significant change or addition to the organization's infrastructure (i.e., new process, method, training, metric, reward, or even tool).

## 2.3 Requirements Documents, Usability, and Teamwork

Many times, software engineers and developers hesitate to get involved with issues related to product requirements. Software developers are sometimes only motivated to write specifications after realizing that the product will not be complete until all required functions are finished. This means that features are documented, integrated, tested, packaged, and released (all workproducts). To accomplish this goal a functional specification must be developed. The functional specification becomes the vehicle by which agreements for excellence are made for team accountability [IMPA96].

Product complexity and functionality are typically in direct opposition to usability. Therefore, simplicity is the key to successful product requirements, designs, and code. This means that the customer use-model for accomplishing each task is clearly identified and documented. Use-models are developed using task analysis and usability testing (e.g., hidden cameras, one-way windows, storyboards, post-it (R) notes, and paper prototypes). Each requirement is carefully numbered so that it can be traced throughout the development life cycle. A numbering scheme also allows a checklist and suite of test stubs to be quickly assembled and shared by all team members [WILS95].

Project success is measured after beta testing is complete. This means that when no user-interface or use-model changes are required, the product is ready. In other words, customers and users can focus on their needs, instead of searching for problems to match solutions provided by the product. Technology is best when it is perceived as a transparent means to an end by the user—a solution. When the product becomes invisible, that is always a good measure of success (from a usability and design perspective). Successful project teams always search for better ways to deliver complete solutions, not just more source code or features.

## 2.4  Requirements Specifications (Fuel for Project Teams)

Successful project teams always strive to have detailed requirements and functional specifications before trying to produce a function or feature. For Graphical User Interface (GUI) software you must always have a detailed design specification (a document which identifies all state transitions). The specification is best when it is written by the developer and reviewed by other project team members. Make sure to have the specification reviewed by the entire project team (i.e., QA, documentation, marketing, technical support, and training).

It is best to include all test methods and procedures directly in the functional specification or design documentation, instead of in a separate document. This way you ensure that test procedures and requirements are always synchronized. Also, remember that a prototype works better than a text description of a function when a model of a graphical user interface is developed.

## 2.5  Total Team Involvement (Tech Writers and Marketing)

Successful project teams are able to obtain and maintain the total involvement of everyone on the team (for example, the technical writer may propose changes to the product use-model). Allowing all members to participate in various product development tasks is extremely useful for building team synergy. Have the technical writers work side-by-side with developers as the product is defined, designed, and developed.

In general, training and treasuring senior technical writers is extremely important to providing successful products. Production editors are key individuals who communicate directly with the user through the documentation. The product documentation provides the first impression (introduction to the software). Training material is just as important as product documentation. Some customers use video training materials to learn how to use the product. This is the first impression the customer has of the company. You only get one chance, so the training material must work.

Technical writers are not only responsible for hard-copy documentation, but all on-line material (product notes, help pages, and solutions to difficult problems). Technical writers provide key data to the user when necessary (both high- and low-level detail). Context-sensitive help (accomplished by clicking on a button for a particular function) is another key deliverable of technical writers.

Technical marketing typically performs many general tasks and functions which include engineering, QA, documentation, and technical support. In fact, marketing does more than just specify the product, they actually help build many of the product deliverables (pieces). Some of the many workproducts provided by technical marketing groups include demonstration files, documentation, benchmarks, and tests. Without the total involvement of everyone on the project team, success is limited, when it is achieved.

## 2.6  Cross-Functional Boundaries

Successful project teams require everyone to successfully work across organizational and functional boundaries. Therefore, successful project teams are comprised of individuals who have the attitude of: "We make sure that this is the best product available." This is in opposition to: "I just do my job. I just work here. I do not own the company." Successful project teams are able to engage everyone in a complete team effort (teamwork), regardless of the geographic barriers (i.e., time and distance).

## 2.7  Reviews (Good Team Practices)

A common challenge to the project schedule is to ensure that everyone on the project team adheres to good quality practices throughout the development process. Best practices for quality begin by doing a review of the existing source code, design, or better yet, requirements workproducts. Code reviews are excellent tools for removing many of the obvious bugs before integration and system testing. Source code reviews also provide the opportunity (before or during the review) to redesign critical code. Proper redesign makes the product more efficient (e.g., performance, usability, interoperability, portability, maintainability, reliability, and scaleability). Successful project teams provide an open and friendly environment for peer reviews and walkthroughs. Reviews also foster sharing of best practices between team members. See the chapters on design and code reviews for further details.

## 2.8  Marketing and the Business Plan

With most new projects, engineering must take a role in championing and supporting various marketing-related issues. Everyone must understand and learn the importance of having a firm marketing roll-out strategy (i.e., business plan). After all, marketing deliverables are also key factors to achieving project and product success. Customers never purchase just source code. The business or marketing plan must include product packaging, licensing, pricing, market position, maintenance, support, performance, functionality, reliability, and other critical factors for success. The product requirements document is the foundation on which engineering functional requirements, architectural documentation, design and ultimately source is developed and tested. The product requirements document also provides a vision toward which the project team can drive.

The product requirements document is best when it is integrated with the organization's strategic business plan (18- and 36-month long-range goals for the corporation). It is also important to have quarterly reviews of key projects and to update and maintain the business and marketing plans. These documents are no different than a functional specification or design document—they must be maintained.

Successful teams are aggressive in getting marketing-related issues resolved up front (functionality, performance, compatibility, and reliability). This is opposed to having people working around the clock and on weekends without knowing the product release date, direction, or roll-out plan. The entire development process must start with a well-defined vision (the marketing and business plan).

## 2.9 Conclusions

- Requirements and functional specifications are the fuel for successful cross-functional teams.

- Successful cross-functional project teams consistently query both sides for status and expect a response within 24 hours.

- Best practice project leaders solicit ideas from each individual and streamline all feedback into the smallest set of proposals possible. Once the team is assembled, one proposal is selected. Successful leaders never flinch in the middle of a storm (crisis).

- The best technology, computing resources, and individual contributors in the world will never replace or substitute the power of a strong cross-functional team.

- Successful project teams always search for better (innovative) ways to deliver solutions, not just more source code or features.

- Functional teams realize that everyone on the project is responsible for success, not just the leader or manager. These teams always strive to beat the competition, never teammates or co-workers.

- The success of a product is judged by the quality of all the workproducts—provided or otherwise (i.e., documentation, training, and demonstration programs). Quality and success are rarely measured by just the executable program on a CD-ROM. Success is accomplished by teamwork.

- Successful teams are able to move between projects using a fluid or dynamic approach which is driven by the corporate business model (mission and vision). These teams never rely on or expect a static business structure or model of performing business with customers.

## 2.10 Questions

1. Why is it important to have documentation and development individuals work closely?

2. What are key elements associated with a successful organization infra-structure?

3. Explain some of the many tasks shared by technical marketing and engi-neering?

4. Why is teamwork so important to project and product success?

5. Why do requirements and functional specifications improve teamwork?

6. Why is it always best to review workproducts early in the development life cycle as a team, rather than later?

7. What are some benefits of numbering functional requirements?

8. List some of the many attributes of a successful project team.

9. What are some team-oriented best practices for quality?

10. What are key attributes of a business plan written for team success?

# Project Teams and
# Quality

# 3

There are a number of ways to measure product quality (e.g., customer satisfaction surveys, code complexity, number of product interfaces, defect density, customer visits, changes in profit—revenue minus costs, and many others). One common method of measuring quality is to measure the number of incoming problem reports from internal and external customers. A fairly flat or declining incoming rate of problem reports is the common goal, however, declining problems may also mean that testing or customer use has simply slowed, or even stopped. Use a tool, such as, PureVision from Pure Software, Inc. to help identify the situation where new problems are no longer discovered, since testing has ceased. Also, use this tool to ensure that the problem reporting system is used as a proactive, not a reactive approach to quality [WILS95].

Incoming problem reports are usually measured using both *critical* and *important* problems (i.e., a critical problem means that the customer must stop work). Critical problems mean there is no work-around to the problem. An important problem usually means that there is a difficult, but useful work-around to the problem. Most critical problems require a solution within a matter of days or even hours.

This chapter discusses how to use various best practices to improve product quality in a project team setting. The intent of this chapter is to show key areas where the project team must make investments to improve product quality. Many of these investments mean changes to the team and personal software processes that are used throughout the development life cycle.

## 3.1 Vocabulary (keywords)

ambiguity reviews, Application Programming Interfaces (API), architect, Configuration Management (CM), cross-functional team, culture, department manager, functional specification, functional testing, independent, intact team, interdependent, metrics, product support, program managers, project leader, prototypes, Quality Assurance (QA), Quality Control (QC), regression testing, release engineer, structural testing, sustaining engineering, technical marketing engineer, technical writer, test, tester

## 3.2 Specifications

Many developers tell other team members what they believe is expected (functional requirements), using fairly informal methods. However, given the complex nature of most software products, documenting the precise behavior in a requirements specification is extremely difficult. The functional specification is written by the developer prior to any other development activities. Functional specifications are also always considered living documents by successful project teams. You may also consider including what is not included in the product when writing the functional specification. Every statement you (the customer) make in the functional specification is one less decision the developer makes for you.

When the functional specification is maintained and updated by the developer, user documentation will more accurately reflect the actual implementation. Source code, libraries, include files, and other deliverables must also be maintained and updated by the project team for future project and product success.

## 3.3 From Specification and Prototype to User Manual

A functional specification is especially important when public Application Programming Interfaces (APIs) are developed. Specifications are especially crucial when other workproducts are reviewed by the customer (either internal or external). The functional specification is the foundation, or basis for construction of user documentation. The technical writer is responsible for this assessment. Functional specifications are best when they are unambiguous, consistent, and complete so that all project team members (i.e., developers, testers, and marketing), can perform their assigned tasks.

Ambiguity reviews are one excellent technique used during a requirements review. *NOTE:* Tom Gilb's and Michael Fagan's inspection methods are considered more rigorous [FAGA86, GILB93]. Ambiguity reviews evaluate word semantics, acronyms, compound sentences, and parent-child requirement relationships. Several other techniques are available. See the appendix on ambiguity reviews for more details regarding this valuable process that is easy to use.

Maintenance of the functional specification is conducted throughout the development life cycle. Successful project teams maintain all specifications throughout the life cycle, even when the manual is complete. Many developers believe that the functional specification becomes a historical reference when the manuals are complete and the product is released. The problem is that the user documentation is now written using existing (incomplete) functional specification. The functional specification must never go out of date. The functional specification and product requirements must always be maintained throughout the life cycle, even after production release.

Consider using the functional specification and prototype together as a complete project specification. Prototypes show the user interface more clearly than documents. Therefore, prototypes are considered valuable models that show how screens and functions will interact with each other (the product architecture). The prototype describes the reasons for feature interaction much more clearly than the written specification [PRES92].

## 3.4 Roles and Responsibilities

Most developers perform many different roles, in addition to writing source code, for example, architect, project leader, release engineer, tester, technical writer, technical marketing engineer, and product support. Engineers are required to perform data collection and monitor progress, but quality and Configuration Management (CM) (version control of all workproducts) are everyone's responsibility.

Successful project teams are self-sufficient in accomplishing all critical functions. These teams are able to cut through all the red tape and make decisions at the local level—a popular idea today in even the largest companies. Cross-functional teams are the key to success. Successful software organizations are interdependent [COVE88], never independent (a disfunctional project team by definition).

## 3.5 Project Team Leaders (the Glue for Success)

Every project team needs a successful project leader, regardless of the programming environment (structured or object-oriented). The project leader is usually someone other than the manager or product architect. These individuals are important, however, they are usually not enough to guarantee project team and product success. Architects are hard to find and their focus is typically on the big picture (i.e., product interfaces, usability, performance, and databases).

Finding individuals to lead the charge (i.e., project leaders) is one of the most difficult tasks most human resource groups face. Project leaders must have a passion to drive a common vision for the project team (i.e., a common architecture) across the entire product life cycle. The project leader is not the same individual who developed the architecture (in most cases). Instead, she is the one empowered to lead the team to complete the architectural vision. Project leaders are not just granted power to make decisions, they must win the trust and respect of the team. After all, the project leader is the individual who is going to make sure everything works according to the plan. Successful project leaders always consider their task a privilege and an honor which is never taken for granted.

Program managers, on the other hand, are responsible for tracking product and project dependencies, problem report counts, milestone dates, and other project planning and tracking tasks. A department manager also has different tasks from the project leader (i.e., staffing, reviews, coaching, and counseling). A project leader is someone who understands all aspects of the project (e.g., technical details, operational issues, and product competition). The project leader is successful when she is respected by all team members. The team must feel confident that they are being led in the right direction by the project leader.

Technology never compensates for poorly defined procedures and processes, implemented by an arrogant project leader.

## 3.6 Too Many Leaders

Having too many project leaders (self-appointed or otherwise) is worse than having no project leader. You cannot succeed without great people. However, even having the best people is not enough to ensure success. Each individual must function as a member of the team, otherwise only chaos thrives.

Good project teams make life much easier for the project leader. If a problem must be solved, the project leader brings the team together and lets the group determine the solution. Teamwork is only driven through a deep sense of commitment and pride of ownership exhibited by all members of the project.

## 3.7  Project Team Pros and Cons

All of the members of a project team must deal with both the highs and lows associated with a software project (for example, everyone is responsible for fixing their own problems). If you write a piece of code, you must own and support the product like a parent cares for a child.

Sustaining engineering groups that are responsible for fixing other people's problems always make me nervous. How can you expect people to learn from their mistakes (be accountable) when someone else is stuck with all the clean-up work (maintaining and correcting problems)? Sustaining engineering is very demoralizing, especially when a senior developer hands over a poorly written piece of code to a new employee. Many times, a junior engineer is expected to support the old product, while a more senior engineer has the exciting next generation project.

Many companies look for superstars to perform object-oriented programming or design, instead of individuals with a passion for delighting customers with great products. Therefore, a technology, not a customer-oriented mind-set is encouraged. This is wrong. On the other hand, not every aspect of product development is sexy and exciting. However, each function created is critical to the overall success of a product. A product that the majority of customers really enjoy using is probably one of the greatest rewards a software developer and project team member ever experiences.

## 3.8  Strength is Not Always In Numbers

The old saying that there is strength in numbers is not necessarily always true when it comes to software development. The benefit of additional developers usually results in increased communication complexity and coordination, especially when team members are located throughout the globe {BROO82}. The role of a project leader is even more difficult with large teams (i.e., more people require direction). Larger project teams mean greater difficulty with overall performance and efficiency (i.e., time to market). Larger teams require more glue code to tie all functions together into a system.

If you do not have a strong leader to ensure that everyone stays together, teamwork problems grow and become even worse, never better. Moreover, everyone on the team tends to start to scatter with a poor leader. After everyone scatters, communication channels will start to fragment and falter. A manager who does not know how to develop or read code can potentially make the situation even worse, since the manager rarely has the respect of the team (able to help resolve and debug problems in a crisis).

## 3.9 Technical Marketing and Engineering

There is only a fine line between a developer's responsibility and the tasks performed by technical marketing. This means that more mature developers enjoy the benefit of a dual role. Successful developers can direct the future of the product and develop the technology (with the project team's help). In other words, the entire project team (based on a vision from product marketing) determines the best strategy for technical product direction, as well as actual implementation.

## 3.10 Quality is Part of The Engineers' Job

Mature project teams employ skilled developers capable of performing Quality Assurance (QA) and testing (Quality Control or QC) tasks when necessary (always). QA includes measuring and improving processes associated with product development. QC is primarily focused on product assessment (testing).

Multifaceted developers are mandatory, since most product technology is specialized, low-level verification and validation without any assistance is impossible by anyone other than the developer (for example, structural testing and analysis of source code and detailed designs [BEIZ95]). Some of many potential structural testing techniques include function call, call entry/exit, statement, decision, switch 0, 1, and 2, as well as data flow methods [BEIZ84, BEIZ90, BEIZ95, WILS95]. Testing also includes functional testing of the product using the requirements and user documentation. There are many functional testing techniques available (e.g., loop, domain, transaction, state machine, graph, and syntax) [BEIZ90, BEIZ95].

On the other hand, engineers in the quality function look after quality. Looking after quality means the QA engineer is like a co-pilot to the project team leader. This individual helps guide the project and warn others of potential dangers throughout the project life cycle. QA engineers must not be asked to achieve quality independent of the project team. Successful teams use the philosophy that everyone on the project team is charged and empowered with the responsibility of achieving the agreed-on quality standard. Never allow the quality function to move away from the engineer to a group or set of individuals (i.e., do not make the quality manager the sole proprietor for product quality).

Quality is a state of consciousness, a mind-set and culture, not just a bunch of metrics, tests, or statistics. However, these items are still critical for measuring success against a baseline. On the other hand, quality also means meeting customers, wants, needs, and desires. Quality is a core part of every project team member's job. Quality is an outward manifestation of the corporate and project team culture. Counting the number of times a managers says, "I think, I feel, and my gut tells me," is one simple metric for assessing someone who is in control (or not in control). Developing a functional specification and measuring test coverage against this document is a key metric for the project team (functional test coverage). More about functional test coverage is included in the chapter on testing.

## 3.11 Technical Publications

In some cases, technical writers for the project team work directly for the project leader, not a technical publications manager. When given the opportunity to have the technical writer report to the project leader, instead of a technical publications manager, there is often concern about career growth. This is because the writer is now fully engaged in the product-team environment and not necessarily working with other writers. Therefore, the project leader is an excellent product team manager—not just an Research & Development (R&D) manager who also must know about technical publications, writing, artwork, and how to put a book together (in general).

Career growth is critical and matrix management through the use of *intact* and *cross-functional* teams is the key to success. Intact teams are local and do not span functional or geographical boundaries. Local single-function (intact) teams are much easier to manage than cross-functional teams which are spread throughout the globe. Many companies are now developing software around the world with specialists in many vast areas (for example, electronic design, operating systems, distributed processing, networking, languages, database design, and other subjects). Therefore, successful cross-functional teams mean the difference between product success and failure.

Writing a document is more difficult than a software module. Users of a software program rarely get to see the source code, you always see the source when you read a book. Successful teams treat each workproduct with respect (pride of ownership) as if the source code were to be shipped to the customer.

## 3.12  Marketing Practices

Successful project team members and leaders "sell" or distribute their products to other groups within the company. This is even more important when the project team is going to be selling heavy technology (i.e., complex, large, and high-risk functions). This type of technology requires that each member fully understand the market trends and technology transitions. Project teams and organizations working in this environment do not need classical marketing individuals, instead, strong technical contributors are required. The reverse is true of traditional (shrink-wrapped) software development organizations.

## 3.13  Training Material

Training materials and lab exercises are critical deliverables (product) that are planned, designed, and developed by the project team. The product team only uses a small percentage of the trainer's time when both individual and project team goals are in alignment. The project schedule must include development of training material from the start.

Product success requires a strong relationship between the project team and the training organization. Close communication with the training function is especially important for new projects. In some cases, the training instructor wears the QA hat. When this happens, ask the training department the following question:

"You are going to have to teach this product. Are you sure that you have everything you need?" (Always match ownership with responsibility and accountability.) If the answer to the preceding question is no, you know that the training material is not ready. If the training material is incomplete, you cannot release the product.

Most training instructors love the idea of getting involved early in the development or planning of a project, just like developers. Therefore, it is important to have the training instructors develop a plan and set of labs (exercises) that can be used for function and regression testing to ensure that the product continues to operate without failures. Synergy and teamwork (including the training function early in the development process) are by-products of a successful project leader. Technical publications should also be provided on a just-in-time basis.

## 3.14  Motivation and Passion for Quality

Everyone must have a passion for achieving results, however, one person usually acts as the nucleus, or distributor of this motivation and excitement. This individual, or set of individuals, become the conduit used to inform the team. The project leader explains why the project is so important and why the team must believe in the mission. Once the vision is set, everybody ultimately must have a passion for accomplishing the team's project goal(s); otherwise, the vision simply remains that—a vision. Once the project leader has motivated and impassioned the team, the pace for the project must be set and maintained using the lead-by-example method.

## 3.15  Ownership and Quality

Make sure that every team member's name (maybe even the team member's picture) appears in all source code and documentation. Product failures are reduced when source code comments and binary information files contain each member's name. My research showed that problem reports increased after developers were instructed not to include their names in the source code. Product reliability and quality suffer when each team member's name is no longer included in either the product literature, demonstration programs, or source code. Successful developers are never associated with a lousy (poor-quality) product. Many companies now print advertisements with pictures of the entire project team.

## 3.16  The Project Team Quality Philosophy

Quality is based on human attitudes. It is not simply a product of technology. Technology is easy to change. People, on the other hand, are very difficult to change. Especially when the change is perceived as unnecessary or unimportant. The responsibility for quality begins with every employee in the company. If any aspect of the product is inferior, the entire team considers the problem their responsibility. In other words, if a problem is my problem, it is also the group's problem and vice versa. Quality without teamwork is impossible. Teamwork without a quality mind-set (culture) is also impossible.

Quality and price together equal value. The software and computer industry is an extremely competitive business where profit margins are always under extreme pressure (constantly shrinking). Never let anyone tell you that quality is not a distinguishing factor. Quality is the umbrella (along with price and value) from which all purchase decisions are made.

## 3.17 Conclusions

- Source code, libraries, include files, training, documentation, tests, and other items are key workproducts which are always included in the specification. The specification is the fuel for the project.

- Successful project teams maintain all specifications throughout the life cycle, even when the manual is complete.

- Successful software organizations are interdependent, never independent.

- Project leadership is a privilege, never a right.

- When interviewing candidates, always look for individuals with a passion for delighting customers with great products, not individuals who are hot-dogs or wild cowboys.

- Quality is the core part of every project team member's job (a mind-set), not a useless metrics report that is ignored by management.

- The project leader must establish the vision for the team and maintain the pace toward the goal. Successful projects are led by competent leaders, who lead by example (they walk the talk). In other words, they do not check-in code unless it follows the coding standard. They also check-in a unit test (with documentation) as well.

- Quality drives teamwork. Teamwork results in quality products and services. Excellent products are the result of hard work from a dedicated team, and rarely come from sole individuals who "did it their way."

## 3.18 Questions

1. Explain the difference between critical and important problems.

2. Why should data be collected during alpha and beta system testing? What tools are available to perform (automate) this function?

3. What are the challenges and differences between intact and cross-functional project teams?

4. Why is there a strong tie between pride of ownership and asking developers to include their names with each source code comment?

5. Why should the project leader ask the training department to participate in the early stages of product development?

6. Why should the project leader insist that his team use functional and structural test metrics during product development?

7. Name some structural test metrics that were mentioned in this chapter.

8. What are potential problems with a sustaining engineering group?

9. What are some of the attributes of a successful project leader mentioned in this chapter?

# The Phased Approach

# 4

Successful software and hardware projects always use a phased approach for product development. A phased approach includes milestones for product requirements, detail designs, design reviews, code reviews, and incremental delivery. However, all of these workproducts and activities are meaningless without a tight-knit project team. See the chapter on project teams for further details. This team must work together extremely well (especially under pressure) for successful implementation of the phased approach.

## 4.1 Vocabulary (keywords)

automatic test generation, Computer Aided Software Engineering (CASE), COnstructive COst MOdel (COCOMO), Hyper Text Markup Language (HTML), impact, must priority, prototype, risk, task analysis, test harness, throw-away prototype, usability testing, verification

## 4.2 The Phased Approach and Planning

Using a phased approach, the project team is able to achieve high quality without feeling overwhelmed by a bureaucratic process. Planning, of course, is still required for success. In fact, planning is much easier when a phased rather than a big-bang approach to software development is embraced [PRES92].

## 4.3 Verification

*Verification* is the process of evaluating the outputs of each phase prior to determining if they are acceptable as inputs to the next phase [IEEE94]. In other words, are we building the product properly? The purpose of verification is to determine if the outputs of the current phase are acceptable as inputs to the next (for example, if the requirements document is complete, accurate, and unambiguous detailed design work can now start). The phased approach results in built-in verification methods and tools for software development.

## 4.4 Prototypes

Projects start with a prototype (post-it® note, computer throw-away model, or pseudo-code). The prototype is frequently used as a basis or model to better understand the customer's real requirements. Prototypes must be developed rapidly so that the customer may quickly assess results and recommend changes [PRES92]. Task analysis, usability testing, and general product demonstration is performed by using a prototype. Once the functionality for the non-prototype system is determined, project funding is secured. Project funding (e.g., people, equipment, and budget) are followed by requirements and design documentation. Reviews are highly recommended throughout the development process for workproduct analysis. Finally, coding, unit testing, integration, integration and system testing, and installation are performed as phases. See Figure 4.1 for how all these tasks are integrated. The glue (key) for the phased approach is testing, analysis, and review (i.e., verification and validation) sponsored by the project leader.

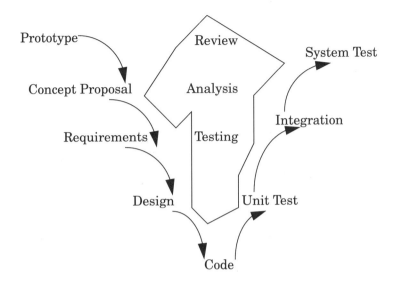

Figure 4.1

A paper or a throw-away prototype is the best place to start the development process after the functional requirements are defined. Prototypes are especially important when a developer is using an unfamiliar subsystem (e.g., a new set of APIs, commands, or GUI objects). The prototype is developed as closely as possible to the environment which is used for product development. One of the greatest benefits of paper and throw-away prototypes is a better-defined set of constraints for the system or function under test. Prototypes allow the developer to "practice," or see how changes and new features impact an existing product design [PRES92].

Always use a prototype to learn and refine the design. If necessary, throw the prototype away and return to the original design. As a result of using the prototype development process you return with much more detailed knowledge and experience. Always design from what you really need, not from what is "perceived" or desired for a subsystem (e.g., APIs, GUIs, libraries, and commands).

## 4.5  Working Within Phases

Successful developers know that it is critical to prioritize all features and functions for the project from the start (for example, must-priority features and requirements are phase 1). Other must-rated items are included in phase 2 of the release cycle. Having agreement with marketing regarding product functionality contained in each product release is critical. Do not start coding until you have completed this agreement.

When phase 1 is completed on time, the team starts working (full-time) on phase 2. Using a phased approach for product development pays several dividends. One reward is the added incentive for new development when the current development assignments are complete and correct (based on the functional requirements specification). The phased approach requires the project team and marketing to agree on the majority of deliverables for each phase at the very beginning of the project (i.e., good forecasting and planning skills are mandatory for success).

## 4.6 Documentation (Text vs. Document Processors)

Documentation is a vital part of the phased approach; however, product packaging must not overwhelm the contents of the design. In other words, never get too involved in making sure that the documentation is pretty. Instead, focus on making sure that every design is testable, readable, unambiguous, and consistent.

Except for architectural design documents (which you may use a document processor to complete), use an ASCII editor or Hyper Text Markup Language (HTML)* for documentation. Text-based tools make electronic mail and other methods of information distribution during product development much easier to accomplish and manage. (I hate it when someone sends me a PC-based application file which I cannot read with my UNIXtm workstation).

The high-level document does not turn into source code. Therefore, it can remain in a document processing system or word processor. Several Computer Aided Software Engineering (CASE) tools exist to help develop design documentation from requirements and source code (for example, DISCOVER from Software Emancipation Technology, Inc.). This tool allows documentation changes to flag required source code changes and vice versa [WILS95].

---

* Tools such as **mosaic** or netscape provide hypertext links that are extremely valuable for organizing, distributing, and sharing specification information.

## 4.7  Changes and Documentation

It is critical that R&D discuss architectural or design changes with marketing, technical publications, training, and other members of the project team. The project team must determine the potential impact and risk to the project for each and every proposed change (requirements, design, source code, test, documentation, marketing, technical support, and training).

The phased approach (for highly technical products) is used to establish a process where engineering provides the initial documentation to technical publications. Technical writers then use the existing engineering documentation as a base to create reference, tutorial, support, and user documentation. (This process requires functional specification maintenance throughout the entire development life cycle.) Some of the many tasks which are performed by technical writers include:

- Adding examples (also useful for automatic function and regression testing).
- Expanding the content to match the implementation as it grows and changes.

## 4.8  QA Involvement—Early or Late?

Another common problem is that the QA engineer is uncomfortable using a staggered release process. However, if you break a project into smaller components, the entire effort is much more manageable. Therefore, it is best to tell QA engineers, and other project team members, when to expect specific packages. The order in which QA engineers should expect to receive each package (product, library, or function) is critical to project success. Many QA engineers only want to test a complete system, not a piece of a product. This makes sense when QA engineers are expected to only perform system testing. However, successful project teams involve all project team members early in the development life cycle (requirements, design, and coding). This way, late surprises are avoided, or prevented altogether.

## 4.9  Specifications, User Interfaces, and Testing

Consider writing the preliminary functional specification as early as possible, even before you know all the details associated with the project. In other words, spend as much time as possible outside the project working on the specification until it is approved. Complete specifications result in valid (accurate) schedules. Maintaining the functional specification from the onset is especially important, since most project team members are usually working on multiple full-time projects in parallel. Also, develop the verification and validation (test) plan in parallel to the functional specification, and review both documents together.

Many projects are separated by core functions and user interfaces. These separations may result in two major architecture documents which attempt to cover all areas. Each architecture document can add complexity unless tight coupling is provided (for example, many development managers think that user interfaces are easy to develop). The misconception is that user interfaces do not require any significant amount of time for design, development, and documentation. Unfortunately, user interfaces require extensive documentation which is not required for complex algorithms and data structures. Graphical user interfaces require comprehensive testing, using state machines, control-flow techniques, task analysis, and usability testing [BEIZ95].

Another best practice for developing and testing user interfaces (from my experience) is accomplished with TestMaster (previously known as MRT) from Teredyne. This tool allows you to model all application states and transitions based on the functional specification which it uses to automatically generate test cases. The test cases are generated as scripts for any test harness such as XRunner, WinRunner, TestDirector, and QApartner {WILS95]. TestMaster determined that one new GUI-interface required 1,000,000,000,000 test cases for constrained path coverage (each loop was restricted to 3 iterations). Obviously, not all of these tests were executed. However, this project ended up selecting a set of tests that provided leaf-level coverage. The end result was that to generate approximately 10,000 tests after a minor change to the product, only a few minutes were required to update the models. Automatic test generation technology really starts to pay back during the product maintenance phase. Who knows how many months it would have taken to develop a new suite of 10,000 tests.

GUI-interfaces are not easier to develop and test, in many cases they are more difficult to validate than commands and library functions. The good news is that after you have completed the models (state machines) from the functional specification, you can have massive amounts of automated tests and coverage. Fortunately, TestMaster has an internal language called Path Flow Language (PFL) which constrains the total number of test cases.

Development of a use-model is one phased approach to solving the problem of an almost infinite number of test combinations within reasonable time restrictions. Random (Monte-Carlo) generation of test path combinations within a GUI is another approach. Finally, switch 0, 1, or 2 methods are another approach to testing GUIs and other control-rich applications (currently not implemented in TestMaster). Switch 0 coverage strives to test each leaf-level function (e.g., each button and object is visited at least once). Switch 1 coverage tests all combinations only from the first level of control flow. Switch 2 coverage expands this coverage to the second level of control flow [WILS95]. System tests should always be developed during the requirements phase of product development. Interface tests are developed (defined) during the design phase. Finally, unit tests are developed during the code development phase. The V-model is one method that is recommended for phased development of tests [WILS95].

## 4.10  Function Separation

Segmenting functions during the design phase helps to lay out the guiding philosophy for code development. This means that functionality is divided into families (a hierarchy). In other words, commands, GUI, and API families are grouped together. Within a command family there may be a read function sub-family for reading a database. There may also be a write function sub-family for database writes. Coding and implementation occur much faster after function partition, since each subsystem has its own detailed design specification (i.e., command family). Testing is also more successful (unit-, integration-, and system-level) when the phased approach to compartmentalizing functions is used.

## 4.11  Technical Publications and Training

Working with technical publications and training functions more closely provides many rewards. Once everyone is comfortable working together closely, the project leader is more confident when the development work is truly complete. (This includes documentation and training material that is ready—at least a first-draft version.) With the phased approach, technical publications and training are viewed by the team as very valuable partners (i.e., providers of very visible parts of the product). Define the user interface early in the development life cycle so that documentation and training engineers can start their work early in the phased development process.

Some QA functions have been told not to start testing until the code is complete. This is due more to culture than anything else (the way things have always been performed). Therefore, when the code is finally complete, there is typically a long ramp-up time required for the QA engineers to finally understand the product and initiate functional testing.

Developers must always want to work closely with all functional group members. Never allow anyone to start "throwing tapes or floppies over the wall." Most project team members always prefer engagement early in the project (ideally, from the very beginning, not at the end—catch up). Throwing tapes over the wall only isolates members of the team and breaks down important communication flow. A phased approach requires excellent cross-functional team member communication and engagement from the start of the project. There is no substitute for engagement and communication between team members.

## 4.12  Training and Design Specification Leverage

Another important best practice is to leverage the work of other groups (for example, training and R&D engineers must work closely together to accomplish their tasks). Training material is best when it is built from a customer use-model (method of performing a task). Training lab material which cannot be completed successfully is usually a good indication that something is wrong. Ease of learning or using a product has its beginnings in the requirements, design, and implementation phases (or lack of them).

The training function usually has direct knowledge from the customer regarding existing products and missing requirements. Successful developers realize that type of customer information and knowledge is key to project and product success. Make sure to include your training instructors in all aspects of product development (i.e., from concept through first customer shipment—all phases of development).

Another benefit of the phased approach is that you can automate the development and execution of training lab material earlier in the cycle. Training labs (exercises) also provide excellent input to function and regression test libraries. Capturing and promoting best practices means that you and other members of the project team never have to reinvent the wheel (i.e., perform a task which someone else has already performed).

## 4.13  Measuring Success

The success of a project is easily measured by the types of questions which are provided by users. Questions such as: "How do I do this?" or "I would like it to do this" are always much better than, "I tried to do this and it did not work." Task analysis and usability testing help drive these types of improvements and are key parts of the phased approach.

Measuring the number of incoming and outgoing problem reports is one of the most frequently used measures of success. Preventing problems in the first place is always much better than having to repair a critical failure after product release. The phased approach is more concerned with preventing problems than with detecting them late in the process.

Successful *cross-functional* and *intact* teams both require individuals who are engaged in the project full-time. Cross-functional teams are comprised of individuals from multiple disciplines (functions) such as QA, marketing, training, technical publications, and engineering. Intact teams are comprised of individuals from the same discipline. It is always best when team members do not continually have to tear themselves off the current project to fix problems with a previous product. This type of planning and process rigor makes the difference between valuable key contributors or puppets who are simply jerked around at the whims of management. Use a tool such as CodePlan from Azor, Inc., which is based on the COnstructive COst MOdel (COCOMO), to develop schedules based on historical data—never hunches [BOEH81, WILS95].

## 4.14 Conclusions

- A phased approach means all members of the project team are involved (invited) to participate at each phase throughout the entire development process. This includes QA, training, marketing, engineering, technical support, technical publications, and other functions as needed (i.e., sales, customers, and finance).

- Always know who your customers are, both internal and external, to measure success throughout the project life cycle and at each phase.

- Project teams using a phased approach are able to measure success much easier (if the previous phase is not complete you cannot continue to the next).

- Training and technical publications are important customers for developers, especially in the product definition phase. However, these customers also have customers. Therefore, ensure that training and publications both meet their customers, expectations by engaging them early in the project.

- Always identify and get your customers involved early in the development process. If you are not sure who and what your customers need, stop everything you are currently doing and find out their requirements (this is the most critical phase of the phased approach).

- A phased approach is how you expect almost all professionals to perform their work. Why should software engineering be any different? Using individual innovation and creativity are critical to success in a soloist musical contest, but not in developing commercial or industrial-strength software products.

## 4.15 Questions

1. Explain what is meant by the phased approach.

2. What are some benefits of including other team members early in the development of a product?

3. What are some advantages of text vs. non-text documents in the cross-functional (global) development environment?

4. Explain the relationship between the phased approach and verification.

5. What are the different types of prototypes that are useful as part of the phased approach to product development?

6. What are some testing methods that should be considered for testing graphical user interface software?

7. What are three methods for reducing the test set selection for testing a complex graphical user interface?

8. During what phase should system tests be developed?

9. When should interface tests be defined and developed?

10. Explain the purpose of switch-level 0, 1, and, 2 techniques.

# Design Specifications

# 5

**M**ost R&D organizations write functional specifications, however, they are informal, ambiguous, and inconsistent. This means that instead of using a rigorous standard for requirements and design specifications (e.g., IEEE), maybe a few bullets on a single slide are prepared prior to a kick-off meeting. The trouble with this approach starts when the team must actually implement (write code) according to the (nonexistent or incomplete) design specification. As a result of missing or poorly written design specifications, engineers go off in their own direction and do what they want, or think they should do. This is really dangerous, especially if no one is reviewing other people's functions to ensure interface compatibility. Top-down reviews are one of the best by-products (benefits) of having functional specifications and design documentation. More will be said about design reviews in a later chapter.

## 5.1 Vocabulary (keywords)

architecture, bubble charts, chunking, code comprehension, code fault, control flow, data transactions, design models, extended finite state models, hacking, Halstead Software Science, index, interfaces, McCabe Cyclomatic Complexity, outlines, re-partitioning, software design, Total Quality Management (TQM)

## 5.2 The Design Model

The design documentation contains models of how the software will satisfy functional requirements. This model includes both data and control flow. For data flow, bubble charts are used to depict all data transactions and transforma-tions. For control flow, charts and outlines are used to depict how control is passed from one function to another (at a high level). The design documentation is also necessary to fully understand how each input is processed to produce out-put.

Several tools now provide the ability to take raw source code and generate data and control flow graphs (e.g., DISCOVER from Software Emancipation Technologies, Inc.). This tool also allows developers to re-partition existing code that was poorly designed to provide a more structured (modular) design. Other tools allow the developer to generate the design model from the functional speci-fication using a state transition editor (e.g., TestMaster from Teredyne).

Regardless of the technology used, design models must be developed to depict how the product will implement the requirements defined in the func-tional specification. It is also important to have a design model of the software so that other developers and team members can understand and review each func-tion's complexity. Several methods (metrics) are available for analyzing design and code complexity (e.g., Halstead Software Science, McCabe Cyclomatic Com-plexity, McCabe Essential Complexity) [WILS95].

## 5.3  Writing Code vs. Specifications

Developers are troubled by having to create a design specification, since instead of writing code (remember there are always tight deadlines), they must now stop and think about how to implement functional requirements (i.e., create a design specification). Software developers place documentation in the same category or priority as doing their income tax. Not only do they dislike the task, it is put off until the very last minute.

Developers must force themselves to create a design specification. Usually after the first couple of days, however, it starts to seem simpler (a natural part of the development process?). Once they start thinking about the design details early in the development life cycle, most engineers realize that software design is really no different than the way many tasks are performed in life. For example, if you are going to repair a bathroom faucet or toilet, you always make sure that you have identified all the required parts before leaving the house for the hard-ware store, don't you? If you do not plan well you end up making many trips to the hardware store and the net result is that the entire project ends up taking much more time than was first expected. Can you image how difficult it is to build a house without a blueprint? The same is true of software development; yet many companies foster and promote a cowboy* attitude toward software development. This type of culture is quite destructive, since it says: "Only a sissy takes the time to write a specification—real developers just write code." Building products without specifications is like building a house on the sand, the first big storm (wave of customer use) only results in a wave of problems and customer dissatisfaction.

## 5.4  The Devil Is In The (Design) Details

One of the most important benefits of spending time developing the design specification is that the documents, models, diagrams, and pseudo-code really help developers design and organize their overall process. One of the biggest difficulties of doing design specifications is that once you start the process, it is very difficult to keep from performing the actual implementation (i.e., writing the source code). This process can become like quicksand, so watch out. Once you start coding too soon, you start finding defects in the implementation. Now you have to start correcting (i.e., cobbling and hacking) the code so that it fits together properly. By the time you get done with the project using this method, it is so difficult to extend the functionality, the only choice is to start all over. This method also makes it much more difficult to maintain the product (e.g., apply corrections and enhancements). Focusing on the detailed design specification up front ensures that most major issues get resolved. Therefore, when it comes time to actually start implementation (coding), the process is much more straightforward and successful (i.e., the product architecture and interfaces are well defined and useful for implementation—coding).

One common problem is that the time consumed in developing the detailed design specification is more than the overall time saved during code implementation. Coding is really just the assembly phase of product development. If you have good instructions coding goes much faster. (Have you ever tried to assemble a model airplane or car without the instructions?)

## 5.5  Culture and Philosophy for Designs

Successful project team meetings focus on team culture and philosophy (for example, how the team wants to approach training, designs, design reviews, and testing. In other words, how to design and develop unit, function, integration, system, beta, and acceptance tests [BEIZ90, BEIZ95, WILS95]. Successful project team meetings are also working meetings as opposed to status meetings.

---

* I do not have anything personally against cowboys, country music, or other like entities.

(Always discuss status-related issues informally before each meeting.) Project team meetings which require each member to reiterate a weekly status report will only degrade morale.

Empowerment is an overused and abused term, however, it is extremely vital to the success of the project. Each person on the project is responsible for the workproducts which are produced (including design documentation). Publicizing personal ownership is one of the best methods to ensure continuous quality improvement (i.e., higher-quality products and services).

## 5.6 Design Specifications and Synergy

Another major benefit of doing detailed design specifications is that other members of the project team are better able to implement different pieces of the design. This also reduces the overhead of constant meetings which are used to clarify who is doing what, since the implementation now comes directly from the specification. If the goal is to release higher-quality products to market sooner, you must have a detailed design specification. Once you have the design specification, various functions are then distributed to different members of the project team. The design specification is the road map for how to build the product [PRESS92].

Design documents are always best when there is a proper balance between structural detail and functional abstraction. In other words, the design document references the functional specification frequently, but does not repeat the content. When possible, always error slightly on the side of detail in the design document (more is usually better than less when it comes to implementing a software design). Design specifications contain many of the procedures found in product pseudo-code. Use an index and table of contents for design documentation to assist new employees and other team members to better comprehend the design. An index and table of contents simplifies the review process—chunking is easier (provides improved code comprehension).

## 5.7 Schedule Savings

One project reported that the total time required for the design specification was approximately two weeks (based on an eight-month project). In this case, the developer felt that at least two weeks were saved during the implementation phase (unit code and test), since the design specification was developed prior to coding. Many developers believe that there are far fewer problems detected when design specifications are used, since the bugs are not put in the code from the start (i.e., code faults are prevented, rather than detected during testing).

The net result of design documentation is a significant savings (several weeks) in total project time (i.e., time to market). Obviously, each code fault [IEEE94] is detected and contained during function, integration, and system testing (in an ideal world). However, if you are looking for higher code quality, maintainability, and extensibility, most successful project teams agree—requirements and design specifications are the answer. When the time comes to extend product functionality, you are sure that the next new or enhanced function is not cobbled together because it was planned via the design documentation. The end result is code that is not difficult to change, since it flows well (i.e., a clean architecture results in solid interfaces—the weakest part of any software system or application).

## 5.8  Ahead of Schedule with Design Specifications

Many projects report that coding time is faster than the original schedule when design specifications are used prior to code implementation. In one case, one team allocated eight weeks for a database function and it ended up being completed in just three. This was attributed to the fact that when the team did the high-level design document, they saw commonality. As a result, a core system was designed which was table-driven (nonlinear). This was different from what the developer originally thought would occur during the development process (a flat file or linear system).

One of the nice benefits of being ahead of schedule is the freedom and flexibility of selectively scheduling additional work. This means that the team can choose to accommodate the wants and desires of customers using the system early in the product development life cycle.

The initial hassle (concern) in using a phased and design approach is the question: "Where is all your code?" However, this request goes away once the team starts to produce source code which has fewer failures than any other project.

## 5.9  Keeping the Design Documentation Updated

Many developers feel that there is no gain in keeping high-level designs updated. The reasoning is that design documents are believed to be fairly static. The true underlying reason usually is that the developer is not really interested in going back and updating the document. (Priorities speak for themselves.) Unfortunately, without updated designs, the product implementation can and does no longer truly reflect the documentation.

Here is a question to ask at this point: "How do you perform verification and validation testing without updated requirements and design documentation?"

Another rationalization for not updating high-level designs is if the documentation is perceived to be reasonably good. If this is the case, the project team is believed to already understand the design philosophy and general architecture. Wrong! Poor communication is one of the biggest contributors to errors. Errors result in coding faults and execution of a source code fault can result in a program failure [IEEE94].

Design specifications are best when all interfaces among team members are structured into modules and compartments for clear product architecture definition. Managing interdependencies is probably the single most complex aspect of software development. Without design documentation that is well structured (developed in stages and phases), you are dead.

## 5.10  Standards for Design

The IEEE standards provide a good backbone for developing a checklist for the creation of either an outline or template for the entire development process (including the design phase) [IEEE92]. However, you must always evaluate each standard carefully and ensure that a degree of flexibility is provided during introduction; otherwise, it is very easy for the team to become overwhelmed. In other words, use what you need and make sure to keep the guidelines flexible enough so that the documents can live and grow with the organization and team. It is important that the project team members use what they feel is appropriate and discard the items in the standard that do not appear useful (at least at the current maturity level).

## 5.11 The Design Phase and Testing

During the detailed design phase, creation of the design specification is an excellent time to think about how to test all workproducts (i.e., documentation, source code, on-line help, and packaging). In fact, it is best to define the tests which are used to verify and validate product functionality and document these tests directly in the design specification. As is the case with the product implementation, the test implementation is more successful when all test designs are defined and documented in the design specification. A sure sign of success is when the QA function would like to adopt R&D unit tests, or visa versa, and migrate them into the automated regression test system (with some embellishment of course). Since the design specification already contains details regarding test purpose, inputs and outputs, training other project team members how to use and execute your tests is much easier. Proper test design is especially critical when complicated code is tested (i.e., detailed design documentation is prepared).

## 5.12 Design Detail vs. Code Size

The number of lines of code written often increases in direct proportion to the lack of detail contained in the design and architectural specifications.* One of the most difficult challenges to the development of the design specification is the level of detail provided. Many teams encounter a "break-even" point where the more detail that is provided, the less benefit that is realized. This obviously becomes very subjective and is difficult to determine.

## 5.13 Right Things Right the First Time

Total Quality Management (TQM) is best summarized as doing the right things right the first time. This means that communication is a key component of success. Documentation and training are also vital to improving quality. Use standard tools and methods for software development (this includes creation of the detail design specification). Do not let your project team members simply go off on their own and start coding (hacking, cobbling, and bending). Instead, start with a sample template or outline for a functional specification. After a review of what the product is going to do, make sure a design specification is developed to describe how the product works (e.g., data transactions, transformations, error and exit codes, data structures, and interfaces). The key is to get developers to

---

* More glue code is required, since integrations and function interfaces were poorly defined from the start of the project.

write it down (the design) and engage other project team members in the review process. Document the knowledge to properly share the benefits among everyone on the team and in the company.

TestMaster from Teredyne Software is a product that allows the developer to develop models of the functional requirements using a state transition editor. Once the extended finite state machine models are developed, TestMaster generates functional tests automatically. Extended finite state models are based on the principle of state machines with the added benefit of history [WILS95]. These object models provide a method for developing the design, and also double as the product design documentation. Successful developers leverage the object models derived from a tool like TestMaster or StP/T from Interactive Development Environments (IDE) to build solid products [WILS95]. Best practices for design use the results (object models) of Model Reference Testing (MRT, now TestMaster) and Object Model Technology (OMT—StP/T) to help project team members during the examination of a complex design. These tools are especially suited for designs which are transaction-based (e.g., a control-rich environment, such as a GUI-interface application) [BEIZ95, WILS95].

## 5.14 Conclusions

- You must know not only what features to provide, but how you will do it prior to implementation (coding). In other words, you must create and maintain the design specification, like them (documentation) or not!

- Once you have taken the time to develop the design specification, you will realize that it is similar to the way that most tasks are performed in life.

- Design documentation is not only a road map, it provides the basis for team communication and function commonality.

- Design documentation provides a medium for team synergy (e.g., product and test design reviews, planning, estimation, and scheduling improvements).

- Use a tool such as TestMaster to develop models (design documentation) for improving the development process. These models define state machines (the sequence of events to perform a task), which also serve as the design documentation. The icing on this cake is automated tests which are provided as a result of developing the models.

## 5.15 **Questions**

1. What is the purpose of design documentation? Why is it so important to the overall software development process?

2. What is one of the primary causes for coding faults and program failures? How can design documentation help eliminate this common source of error?

3. Explain the purpose of a design model.

4. Why is it useful to include test descriptions directly in the design documentation?

5. What are some of the biggest (most common) obstacles most people face when design documentation is suggested? What are some potential solutions to these problems?

6. Why is the design documentation considered a road map?

7. Name some representative ways (methods) of depicting the design model.

8. What are some of the many tools that are useful for developing design documentation from a functional specification?

9. Why is team culture so important to project and product success?

10. What are some examples (methods) of a sound team culture?

# Design Reviews

# 6

**D**esign reviews are just one of many best practices for software engineering. Design reviews identify design errors in the development life cycle as early as possible. The review process starts by having one team member distribute a design document to the team. After examination, the team holds a meeting to discuss the design document package. During the discussion the team reviews the document for understanding (top-down review), correctness, completeness, ambiguity, and verification (bottom-up review).

This chapter describes how reviews are used effectively by project teams. Discussion also centers around tools and techniques used throughout the software development process, not just designs. You and your project team should find many of these techniques useful for integration with your company culture, environment, and goals for quality improvement. Given the choice between design and code reviews, the greatest return on your investment comes from design reviews. This is because the cost of performing a design review is substantially less than for a code review. A successful design review also means that unnecessary, incomplete, or incorrect code is never written and then thrown away or reworked.

## 6.1 Vocabulary (keywords)

buddy system, defect repair, design, examination, inspections, interfaces, mentor, moderator, peer reviews, recorder, reviewer, reviews, return on investment, shared memory, team building, top-down

## 6.2 The Design Review

The design review is a critical task for product and process success. Reviews provide the necessary information for the developer to analyze and evaluate the product. During a review, it is best for the project leader and author to jointly decide what to do and what not to do. Successful design reviews provide an open forum for all members to learn and grow in their design experience and expertise. Another major by-product of the review is team building. Successful design reviews provide the opportunity to improve the project team and individual interpersonal communication skills. Successful reviews, like successful executives, always look for multiple benefits and rewards from a single change (high leverage).

Design reviews with key peers from other project groups are also critical to success. Internal consumers of the product are the best source of feedback. Consumers can point out architectural and functional issues that are extremely difficult to capture in isolation. The most frightening thing I have seen is when a developer is told to go away and write the xyz function. Three months later, she crawls out of her office (like a prisoner removed from solitary confinement). Now she is asked by the project leader to check-in her code to the system. This action results in complete chaos, as many working functions now no longer operate, or even build.

Reviews for understanding (top-down), provide a significant increase in code reuse. Top-down reviews provide architectural and interface structure without low-level details. Source code, binary and functional compatibility are all critical to the design, as most customers want the greatest investment protection possible. One of the biggest nightmares most MIS managers face is spending a fortune on a product and then learning that it has now become completely obsolete without any migration or transition path. Design documentation and reviews provide investment protection (more value to customers), as quality is designed in, never tested into a product.*

Design specifications and reviews are important for critical new projects. They are also one way to share best practices between team members. Obviously, it is unrealistic to attempt to provide a detailed design specification for everything. Therefore, it is a good idea to select key new or existing projects based on the relative risk (e.g., customer satisfaction, defect density, complexity, equipment, human resources, and schedule constraints).

---

*Unless, of course, you start the testing process from the very beginning of the project, not at the end.

## 6.3  Design Reviews Goals

Design reviews allow adjustments in the product design and implementation before you have gone too far into development and delivery (i.e., coding and maintenance), since the design is reviewed you actually spend more time making sure that all open issues and problems are resolved prior to the review. Design documents provide a well thought-out and thorough implementation (i.e., complete and correct method of how to accomplish a requirement). Reviews improve code reuse, since project team reviewers suggest existing routines to solve a problem. These routines are used in place of a proposed new function or subsystem.

## 6.4  Reviews or Repair

The flip side of performing reviews is paying for it later (defect repair). If reviews are not performed, chances are that every time you or someone else on the project team looks at source code which somebody else has generated, its style or standard is probably unique (for example, software developers write their own private functions when standards are not applied, since common support routines are not documented and used). This creates redundancy, especially when an in-line function or section of code is used to perform a task that is repeated throughout the code. Instead, the developer should have used an optimized standard function. Program text (source code) that is loaded in shared memory (shared libraries) can make the overhead for a function call practically negligible.

## 6.5  Design Review ROI

Execution of a design phase and the use of design reviews are critical to product and project success. It is very easy to calculate the results (return on investment) of performing a successful design review by measuring the cost to conduct the review vs. the cost of product repair after shipment. To calculate the cost of the review, simply divide the total number of issues discovered by the total estimated dollars to conduct the review. If 45 issues were discovered and the total time consumed for review was 30 hours at $100 a hour, divide $3,000 by 45. The net cost is approximately $66 per issue (typical defect detection rate is 1 to 2 defects per hour). You need to talk to your accounting and engineering people to determine the approximate accounting costs associated with fixing product defects. (I am very confident that the defect repair cost is much greater than $4 per problem.) Most companies average between $5,000 and $10,000 to repair, test, package, and distribute a fix for a release critical problem. However, some of the larger companies are reported to have spent as much as $40,000 to $50,000 per problem. Therefore, you can quickly see the financial advantage of performing a review.

Requirements and design reviews achieve high quality and provide the most bang for the buck. Not all issues that are discovered during a review cost $5,000, or even $50,000 to repair. However, there is always a cost associated with rework (i.e., patch and repair), not to mention customer satisfaction. The hardware world has learned the critical cost associated with rework and has implemented disciplined processes to ensure success. In this regard, software companies must learn from hardware companies. Success is achieved when long-term goals are achieved (quality improvement).

One fact that is usually noticed as a result of performing design reviews is that when the project team has completed the project, they really and truly are finished. Obviously, minor maintenance effort is expected and required. However, significant problem resolution is not required well into the next release cycle.

## 6.6 Flexibility

Flexibility is critical whenever you start a new way of doing development (i.e., designs and design reviews). You can always make changes over time, either more formal or informal (for example, you and the team may determine that doing detailed designs down to the module level is simply not practical). Instead, you may decide to focus only on architectural issues associated with high-level designs. This type of top-down approach is good for both understanding the design and verification (testing) of it. You may want to know what overall design idea was used to create each product or feature in a product family. Once this information is available, the team can better determine which features are included in the design after review. In most cases, the entire system is usually not designed to the same level of detail (i.e., in many cases it is acceptable for some features, or subsystems, to be designed more thoroughly than others).

## 6.7 Cherry Picking Designs (Unique Function)

Only develop detailed designs when the project team believes they are appropriate and beneficial. Successful developers eliminate noise data from their designs such as self-obvious or cookie-cutter routines which contain the same basic framework for the system. If you are developing a series of commands which are similar, but which have different arguments, do not repeat the same logic or function. Instead, eliminate the noise data and procedures in the design documentation so you can better define and establish the real underlying idea.

## 6.8 Group vs. Individual Access

For high-level or architectural designs, the majority of project team members must be involved in the development and review from the beginning (also throughout the project). For low-level designs (modules and functions), a mentor- or buddy-based approach is very successful. Mentors, or buddies, are engineers who work closely with the design engineer to refine thoughts and ideas before they are committed to implementation. A buddy is assigned, or delegated, to help develop and review the design in real-time. The buddy approach is applied for high-level, or architectural designs when the team must operate under a tight schedule.

Use a more formal design review approach early in the development life cycle. This way all appropriate team members are involved in cross-functional verification and communication.

## 6.9 Informal vs. Formal Design Reviews

Informal design reviews work best for teams that are just starting to share (review) each other's workproducts. Developers who are new to the review process sometimes feel less intimidated by an informal review. However, informal reviews lack the structure, rigor, and benefit of achieving a clean design. A proper balance between rigor and making the review a fun activity is the key to success.

Design reviews allow everyone to first self-examine their implementation and potential problems on paper before committing an algorithm or data structure to code and to ensure that the design document is ready to release. During the discussion period, design alternatives are not presented, only problems with the existing design documentation. Design documentation (i.e., control- and data-flow models) provide the means for everyone on the project team (and others) to see things on paper. This in turn reduces the total amount of rework associated with writing source code.

In many cases, design documentation allows the project team to visualize data and process commonality. Therefore, design documents help identify common utility functions. This critical benefit is not available once the project team has started coding.

## 6.10 Design Reviews and Informal Inspections

A reference checklist is used to help developers conduct the review using more structure than what is provided in a simple peer review. Peer reviews are good, however, structured reviews (i.e., a review using a moderator, recorder, reviewers, and a specific plan) are more successful. Structured reviews prevent problems earlier in the development life cycle and have many other benefits. These reviews are less formal than inspections. Inspections require more documentation and administration than a structured review, but are recommended when the maturity of the organization is supportive [FAGA86, GILB93].

Design review checklists are best when they are considered as usable, flexible, living documents. They are also best when customized by each project team member for the maximum possible benefit. The purpose of a review is to produce a better product, not more red tape. However, the goal of a review is to ensure that the design document is ready to release.

The purpose of the following checklist is to provide developers with an instrument that can be used over and over again for high-impact design reviews [FREE82]. The meat of the review is conducted during the private examination period. The planning period takes place prior to the examination phase. This is when the author must choose a moderator, recorder, and at least one reviewer. During the meeting period, the moderator is responsible for conducting the review. The checklist provides a guideline for ensuring a successful review. The moderator and author are both responsible for completing the tasks assigned during the review's follow-up period. In summary, structured design reviews provide the necessary infrastructure for workproduct review in an informal environment.

## 6.11 Design Review Guidelines

- Ensure that the design conforms to the functional specification.
- Validate that the algorithms provided in the design specification are correct.
- Evaluate if a better algorithm should be used for the same solution.
- Determine if the design is modular, structured, or object-oriented (based on

the development methodology selected). Does the design emphasize features such as modularity and reusability?

- Identify if all subprogram interfaces are well defined.
- Determine if the subprogram name(s) are meaningful (for example, is the naming convention followed consistently?).
- While submitting a defect (problem) report, classify the defects according to severity. If the document is line numbered, give the line number (or range of a set of lines).

## 6.12  Design Review Guidelines and Checklist

### Preparation Period

1. The author prepares a package that includes all relevant design documents for review. Requirements documentation is provided as reference information.

2. The author picks a moderator, recorder, and at least two reviewers.

3. The materials are distributed and the moderator sends a meeting notice to the team.

4. The team meets after adequate time has been provided for individual examination (suggested minimum two days, but not more than five).

### Examination Period

1. Does the design help meet project goals (i.e., functional requirements)? If not, why?

2. Does the design implement any unnecessary functions, data transformations/transactions, or operations?

3. Does the design properly address all human factors (usability, testability, reliability, safety, or other critical factors)?

4. Is the design complete, easy to understand, and unambiguous? (See the appendix on ambiguity reviews for details.)

5. Is the design self-contained? Can you write code from the information provided? If not, what detailed information is missing?

**6.** Are external dependencies clearly identified? How about relationships between functions and modules?

**7.** Are all installation, licensing, and packaging requirements complete and tested?

**8.** Are all algorithms, data structures and models, new functions, tables, classes, interfaces, and other design attributes properly identified?

**9.** Are new macros, include files, symbols, and coding conventions identified?

**10.** Are all known and potential exception conditions identified and defined? (This includes errors, warnings, and assertions.)

**11.** Are all operating environments considered? (for example, memory, hard disk, CPU, network, frame buffer, display, compiler, libraries, utilities, and other software and hardware resources).

**12.** Are the following issues addressed (none, some, or all depending on the product requirements-:

[ ] Maintainability. Is the design readable and supportable?

[ ] Reliability. Is the design testable and therefore is the reliability expected to be easily measurable (can you properly test the design)?

[ ] Scaleability. Is the design extensible (e.g., laptop to supercomputer systems)?

[ ] Functionality. Does the design satisfy the requirements defined in the functional requirements and product specifications?

[ ] Compatibility. Is the design compatible with existing designs and requirements?

[ ] Interoperability. Does the design address necessary communication facilities for both data and functions?

[ ] User documentation and training. What is the impact and use-model?

[ ] Security and protection (for example, is data protected or private?).

**13.** Are existing functions used when possible?

**14.** Are storage and performance issues addressed?

**15.** Are all fields described correctly and are any fields missing?

**16.** Are all possible input parameters tested? Also, return codes and parameter formats?

### Discussion Period

**1.** All team members must be prepared to discuss the design.

**2.** The moderator keeps the meeting moving forward.

**3.** The recorder tracks and records issues (metrics collection) [PRESS88, GILB93, GRAD92].

**4.** The author is not intimidated during the review.

**5.** Two hours at most are dedicated to the review, after that a second meeting is scheduled (if agreed on by the team).

**6.** The author's manager is not present at the meeting unless requested.

**7.** The moderator thanks the reviewers and author for a successful review.

### Follow-up Period

**1.** Have all serious problems been resolved by the author?

**2.** Does the team need to conduct a second review?

**3.** Are all minor problems recorded and assigned to an owner? (if needed).

**4.** Are metrics collected and provided to the QA function?

## 6.13 Conclusions

- Design reviews that focus on team building (structure) and quality improvement (inspection) provide one of the best methods of preventing errors. Errors are prevented, since team members communicate how the product is built prior to code development.

- Structured reviews are less formal than formal inspections (less procedures and forms are required). On the other hand, structured reviews provide more rigor than a simple peer review. (A moderator, recorder, and at least two reviewers are active participants during the examination periods.)

- Design reviews ensure that the design is flexible enough to meet the needs and requirements of consumer functions. Interfaces are always the most difficult aspect of software development (architecture). Design reviews are critical to ensuring that everyone is using the same blueprints before coding.

- Having the right people use a checklist (like the one provided in this chapter) during the examination period provides several benefits. Many of these rewards are obtained during the discussion period; however, the majority of the rewards are realized later in the development process (i.e., unit, integration, and system test phases). Training and treasuring individuals who are passionate and committed to reviews is as critical (if not more so) as having a checklist, guideline, or standard for reviews.

- Design reviews are truly one of the most valuable software engineering best practices available. Using the structured review approach (team building approach to workproduct review) makes this process even more successful.

## 6.14 Questions

1. What is the purpose of a design review?

2. What is the role of a moderator in a design review?

3. Who should pick the moderator for a design review?

4. What is the purpose of having a recorder for a design review?

5. What are the three key periods associated with a design review?

6. Why is it important to prepare in advance for a design review?

7. What is the difference between a structured review and an inspection?

8. If an inspection is more rigorous than a review, does this mean that it is always better? Why not?

9. Why is a checklist for a design review a useful tool for success?

10. What is the advantage to the author in using a checklist prepared in advance?

# Code Reviews

# 7

$\mathbf{C}$ode reviews are an excellent best practice for software engineers and developers. This chapter describes how reviews are effectively used by project teams (individuals the author has had the honor to work with over the last 18 years). Reviews are not as robust or rigorous a method as inspections [FAGA86, GILB93]. Therefore, you may ask, how can reviews be considered a best practice? The answer is that very few companies today perform any type of inspection of source code. This chapter discusses methods that can be adopted in the short term. In the long term, more formal methods of code inspection must be adopted and are recommended [GILB93, FAGA76, WEIN90]. This includes many of the tools and techniques which are available for use throughout the software development process (not just during the coding phase). You and your project team should find many of these review techniques useful for integration with your company culture, environment, and goals for quality improvement. Although code reviews are more expensive to implement than design reviews, review of source is an excellent practice for defect containment and failure prevention. It is always better to detect a code fault as a result of a review than to test for failures using functional and structural tests. However, code reviews, functional, and structural testing are all necessary and critical for defect detection and containment. Given a limited schedule and budget (always the case), code reviews are recommended before design reviews.

## 7.1 Vocabulary (keywords)

action plan, bottom-up, checklist, chunking, code reviews, complexity, defect density, design reviews, faults, guidelines, Hierarchical Input Processing Output

(HIPO) diagrams, memory management, metrics, peer reviews, preparation, risk assessment, standards, testability, top-down

## 7.2  Code Reviews (an Introduction)

Most code reviews are bottom-up. This means that the reviewers must be somewhat familiar with the code structure and functional requirements to successfully participate in the review. Preparation for the review discussion is almost always required. In fact, a good review moderator reschedules the meeting if the review team is not prepared. Preparation is the single most difficult obstacle to overcome when trying to initiate code reviews in an organization.

On the other hand, code reviews can also be performed top-down for understanding. Top-down code reviews are more successful (efficient and effective) when the author provides a Hierarchical Input Processing Output (HIPO) diagram of the source code. This diagram assists other team members in understanding the general flow of the source. Many CASE tools now provide both data- and control-flow diagrams from the source code [WILS95].

Successful code reviews generate comments which result in selective (surgical) code changes. The goal of each code change is always to increase, never to decrease, product quality, stability, testability, portability, interoperability, extensibility, functionality, and reliability. Never use code reviews as a forum for nit-picking syntax or static analysis-related problems. There are many tools, such as **lint**, which already provide this service, and usually perform it much better than a human reviewer. Instead, code reviews are more successful (useful) when they identify key functional and architectural problems (e.g., cross-functional dependencies between or within teams). Successful identification and resolution of these types of issues typically can either make or break a project.

Many comments are generated during the examination period of the code review process. A successful project team, with good group synergy, provides many constructive comments during the discussion period. Always remember to help the team strive to eliminate source code faults (bugs) as early in the process as possible (another purpose of code reviews). Also remember that code which is difficult to maintain, or to port to other system platforms is usually a sign of missing coding and porting guidelines (also mandatory for successful reviews).

Detail and preliminary code reviews always have a much higher return on investment than physical product testing (especially ad hoc testing). Architecture and high-level design reviews have an even greater return than ad hoc manual test methods. Most engineering managers place more emphasis on design reviews than code reviews. This is due to the inherent complexity associated with source code. One example of this is when the implementation has not been committed to source code. In this case, function or operation changes are much easier to implement. Another reason for avoiding code reviews is that reading source code is more difficult and time-consuming than examination of a design. A checklist of best practices associated with code reviews is provided later in this chapter to help overcome both obstacles.

Detailed code reviews of Graphical User Interface (GUI) source code is also critical to project and product success. For each GUI code review, consider inviting members from outside the project team (e.g., usability, testability, reliability, performance, and other experts). Appropriate recommendations are then incorporated into the product source code hierarchy. These recommendations are also logged and tracked for future analysis. Successful project teams are never afraid of defining goals and tracking metrics, instead they use this information just as a pilot uses instruments in the cockpit [GRAD92, WILS95].

## 7.3  Code Review Benefits

Code reviews have many benefits similar to those of design reviews. Successful reviews point out poorly documented or hard-to-understand source code. Successful code reviews also allow all project team members to learn new coding methods and techniques (both the author and the reviewer). In other words, reviewers learn new techniques from the author's code. The author also learns new methods and techniques for coding from reviewers (e.g., simpler methods of using a language construct). Successful reviews always avoid getting bogged down with low-impact errors. These issues should be eliminated prior to the review by the compiler or a static analyzer. Successful code reviewers strive to detect documentation, functional, and architectural errors.

One project reported the cost of conducting code reviews to be $25 per issue. This cost was determined by dividing the total number of issues detected by the total number of labor hours required. The burden cost assumed was $100,000 per year for each reviewer (approximately $48 per hour). In other words, approximately two issues were discovered every hour using code reviews.

Some reviewers may provide comments for every line of source code reviewed. In most cases this is overkill. After all, you must make the assumption that reviewers know the syntax and semantics of the language used; otherwise, you have the wrong person reviewing the workproduct. On the other hand, never assume that all source code is self-documenting. Moreover, comments in the form of a Hierarchical Input Processing Output (HIPO) diagram help explain source code flow (i.e., structural control and data transactions and transformation). HIPO diagrams show a hierarchy of inputs and outputs based on the requirements and design specifications. Code which cannot be mapped into the diagram usually has some sort of code structure-related problem.

During a review, consider breaking each function into a sub-block and include relevant comments for each sub-block. Using this technique, other developers and project team members are able to get the gist of what is going on without actually wading through all available code. Whenever more detail is required by the reviewer, the code is usually too complicated. Instead of a code review, structural redesign is required. Alternatively, a separate document is required to describe the algorithm (as implemented) in more detail.

Coding standards and reviews provide the opportunity for everyone to take a second look at the code after the new version is complete. When the code is first written most developers only think in small chunks (i.e., a section, or segment at a time). After the code is complete, developers frequently find global optimizations (e.g., functional consolidation and data structure folding). These optimizations are usually not visible during the actual code development phase. Better yet, look for global optimizations during the design stage for an even bigger return on investment.

Chunking code into blocks really improves code comprehension and makes the code examination phase more successful and beneficial for all parties involved [RIFK95]. Object-oriented programming and design also benefit from the same principles found in most textbooks (i.e., a table of contents, index, glossary, and a synopsis). These entities all provide valuable information for other members of the project team.

## 7.4  Coding Standards and Guidelines

Reviews are also useful for pointing out coding standard issues which are not obvious to the author or to other team members. Selecting a team to champion the creation of a set of code review guidelines benefits both the team and the customer (end user). Coding standards are one of many results and by-products of developing and administering a code review process. Most developers are surprised at the number of existing coding guidelines and standards which are already available within their company. Coding guidelines and standards also help the author and reviewers to prevent portability problems prior to central integration.

Conducting reviews also means that each developer is much more likely to document their code more, since someone is going to have to read and understand what they have written. Self-inspection leads to improved code maintainability and quality, and it occurs more frequently when reviews are scheduled. Successful code reviews are also able to detect and prevent memory leaks and access violations. Tools such as Purify, Insight, and TestCenter are excellent for debugging memory management problems [WILS95].

The days of the obfuscated C programming contest (who can write the most unreadable C program) have now been replaced by the increased competition to provide shrink-wrapped and commercial-grade software products. We now need a best practices C programming contest. These individuals are the real heroes in the organization.

Sometimes developers feel that it really does not matter if the code is compliant with the standard, as long as it "works," that is all that matters. On the other hand, successful project teams have learned that the team must use a common style or standard; otherwise you are doomed to failure. Successful project team leaders know when to reject code; and if necessary, remove an employee from the team. Nobody is ever important enough to write code "their way" and cause the team to suffer as a consequence. Smaller-sized project teams help make this method more practical than large teams. Successful small teams share their code with other small groups. The end result is that standardization, not individualism, is critical for success with any software project.

## 7.5   Consumer Functions are Customer Functions

Usually, the functional specification does not get the proper attention it deserves unless you sit in a review meeting and talk specifically about the document (e.g., what is the product going to do?). Get people to review the functional specification up front and agree on the functionality, and do not allow functionality changes to occur later in the development life cycle. Changing code late in the life cycle typically results in coding compromises and the increased likelihood of coding faults (potential for product failures). Never just tag on another member to a data structure, or change the return code for a function from an integer to a double without significant investigation. These types of changes have serious implications and can very easily break functioning interfaces.

Always treat your consumer functions as you would a customer. After all, consumer functions are developed using a data structure or return code and continue this way unless instructed otherwise. This may sound like common sense.

However, always consider the impact of changing the size or type of a variable for a function prototype. Before you make a change, always consider the impact on all consumer functions (i.e., risk assessment). If you are providing a shared library (programs that reside in computer memory and are used by multiple processes), consider the implications if the program is never recompiled. Always know where and what your consumer expects and treat this as you would a binding legal contract. Always treat source code interfaces (and people) with the upmost care.

## 7.6 Reduced Rework

One primary goal of performing code reviews is to reduce rework (defect repair). Therefore, the time consumed during the review is expected to provide an even greater return later in the development process. The greatest payoff occurs during the testing and maintenance phases of the development life cycle. Always validate and measure the review by asking the following questions:

* Has more code been written than is necessary?
* Has the review resulted in better-defined functionality?
* Are the functional and architectural interfaces more clearly defined?
* Are fewer bugs (source code faults) now resident in the code?

The project team must adjust the project schedule to account for shifts in resources as a result of performing reviews. However, you cannot expect perfection, well at least not at first. In the short term, you may have many old problems that do not get immediately resolved through reviews. However, the next product for release is usually less of a thorn in your side.

Unfortunately, code reviews usually require the pain of a fairly disastrous product release cycle before they are even considered by many project teams. Do not wait until extraordinary effort is required at the tail end of the release cycle to get the product to work. Nobody wants this type of fiasco to happen, yet it is still quite common in many organizations. Fiascoes are not the ideal impetus for process change. Make continuous improvement (process and method change) a goal for everyone on the project team, and ensure that performance reviews take this into account.

## 7.7 A Bad Nightmare

One of the worst nightmares for any project leader is when code that was considered stable and ready to ship falls apart at the last moment (e.g., final integration, or system and acceptance test phase). This usually requires concentrated effort by the entire project team (i.e., extra hours and weekends to get the product ready to ship). Successful project teams learn from their past mistakes and pull together using a lot of cooperation and synergy when nightmares occur. However, successful teams never allow the same condition to occur again.

During the crisis is when you must discuss and identify the root cause of each failure, as well as the best solution, or action plan. This is also the time to discuss ways to improve the code behavior by using informal (peer reviews) and formal (inspections, walkthroughs, and structured reviews) verification methods.

In looking at source code during debug and repair, most developers are amazed at how many problems are prevented by a second or third set of eyes (i.e., code reviews). Code review benefits include the following and more:

- Preventing the potential for "show stopper" problems.
- Detecting both major and minor problems.
- Identifying design flaws earlier in the development process.
- Synchronizing different developers' code and workproducts sooner.
- Educating and orienting developers and project team members with other individuals' code.
- Increasing team motivation for writing easy-to-understand code.
- Strengthening the team's motivation to document the code prior to the review.
- Increasing the awareness of quality and performance criteria, not just functionality.
- Increasing the chance of code reuse, since all the developers are aware of each other's code.

## 7.8 Code Review Prerequisite 1: Preparation

The main cost or penalty associated with code reviews is having to read and understand several pages of unfamiliar source code and spend hours of time discussing what to do next. On the other hand, most reviewers discover that if they spend the time before the meeting to understand the code (the examination period), they remain fully engaged throughout the entire review.

Many developers find the code review discussion interesting and stimulating. On the other hand, when you (the reviewer) simply attempt to "wing it" and not prepare, expect to get lost, bored, and even frustrated. All of these feelings and emotions are pretty much guaranteed, especially when you try to keep pace with the team during the discussion. Preparation is key to a successful code review.

## 7.9  Code Review Prerequisite 2: Management Support

It is especially important that the engineering management team understands the importance of design and code reviews and encourages all project teams to participate. Management support is even more important when a team is under a very tight schedule. Always take the time to perform the review, even if it is informal (e.g., a buddy check or lunchtime discussion).

Code reviews yield many more defects than physical testing (especially ad hoc manual testing). Therefore, consider taking some time from the test phase to do a code review, especially when this phase is primarily ad hoc, as is frequently the case. Treat code reviews as an important component (phase) in the overall software development process (i.e., product verification and validation, or testing across the life cycle). Document and use the results of each code review to notify management that reviews pay for themselves and more. If management does not believe in the review process, then management, as well as the code, is broken and needs correction.

## 7.10  Code Review Prerequisite 3: Standard Coding Style

Establish a standard coding style up front to ensure successful code reviews. Source code styles are very beneficial in producing more readable code, especially when members of the same team are using the same micro-level standards.* In addition to the long-term benefits of more maintainable code, standards and guidelines enable the team to develop and review much more code in a shorter time period (i.e., increased code comprehension).

Code reviews allow the project team to better understand and enhance existing coding guidelines and standards. Remember, coding guidelines form the foundation for code development and must be maintained in parallel with product development.

---

* Start with a corporate guideline and tune the document according to the team's requirements.

## 7.11 Code Review Benefits and Drawbacks

In most all successful code reviews, someone always finds at least one "show stopper" or important problem in the code. By doing an individual code review, developers usually catch problems quickly after they start their personal review. This means that they can go back and correct the code prior to the review (discussion period). Code reviews also find sections of code that are written more efficiently to improve function or system performance. This is especially useful when you are reviewing a significant amount of new code that has not had any extensive function, integration, system, or acceptance testing.

Successful reviews always provide the open opportunity for other team members to learn about the author's development environment (for example, debugging, configuration management, testing, documentation methods, and tools). Code reviews also create a collective intelligence which enables all team members to freely exchange ideas or gain useful insight into solutions to challenging problems. Successful code reviews introduce predictability and controllability into the project planning process. High-impact reviews incorporate best-of-breed coding practices into the development process while enhancing the following:

- Efficiency
- Readability
- Modularity
- Reusability
- Testability
- Usability
- Maintainability

Successful code reviews also ensure that more source code works correctly according to the project schedule, or sooner.

Successful code reviews are measured by the long-term return on investment. All of these attributes combined mean that successful code reviews increase the probability of 100 percent customer satisfaction (i.e., continuous quality improvement).

## 7.12 When To Review

For a new project of any size (especially products with thousands of lines of source code and documentation), code reviews are considered a "given" from the very start (by best practice teams). A review is considered mandatory when a program or module is going to be replaced by a fairly high-maintenance piece of code. This is especially important when the code is enhanced over the years without any significant architecture changes. Unfortunately, maintenance code is very rarely reviewed. As a result, when developers change assignments, the underlying design and structure become obscured, or even lost. One reason for this situation is the fact that most source code is used much longer than initially anticipated or expected.

## 7.13 Reviews and Important Language Features

Learning different or better ways of using new features of a language is another benefit of a code review. One example is when a developer entrenched in Pascal or FORTRAN code for the last several years ends up with rusty C programming skills. Code reviews provide the opportunity to reintroduce developers (and introduce other team members) to the current standards, conventions, and approaches associated with a programming language. New programming techniques are specific to the new target language and environment, but result in a savings of many hours of unnecessary effort. Code reviews are very important for C programmers who are asked to move to C++. Changing languages is often perceived to automatically result in a new development methodology (i.e., structured to object-oriented analysis and design). Unfortunately, this is not always the case.

## 7.14 Informal to Formal Reviews

Most code review processes are usually informal (or at least in the beginning until the culture and maturity of the development community changes). On the other hand, as more and more successful reviews occur, the team is better able to review large bodies of code in a relatively short amount of time.

The process of reading source code is very much like that of reading and writing English. The more you practice, the better you are able to refine your reading comprehension, speed, and accuracy. A significant amount of communication transpires outside of the code review which enables the team to effectively review the code and resolve other issues after, or prior to, the review. This review process also strengthens the bonds (interpersonal and cross-functional communication skills) of the team.

Successful reviews require management support as well as employee dedication. This means that everyone must be dedicated to constantly refining and improving the review process, standards, guidelines, and metrics. Also, make sure to consider project planning and other infrastructure-related issues during a post-mortem of a review.

## 7.15 Specifications and Reviews

Pay special attention to areas of high risk when determining what function or product to review. Also, consider defect density, complexity, testability, and interoperability when selecting a product or function for review (for example, resolve all algorithms and data structure issues early in the design process). Next, determine the complexity of the code and always attempt to simplify the design as much as possible. It is critical for the team to have a good feeling (confidence) that the code can be produced using the current detailed design. In other words, you must completely define the data, algorithms, interfaces, and other design attributes to successfully start writing code. For details, see the design review checklist provided in the chapter on design reviews.

Make sure to invite all appropriate technical experts to a design review for the maximum return on investment (e.g., usability, reliability, testability, interoperability, and other specialists). Having an expert reviewer is extremely valuable and saves time and effort later in the project (e.g., during the integration and test phases). No technology is known today that would replace the human mind and experience which is derived from a technical review. When performed properly, technical reviews provide significant benefits over other commonly used evaluation methods (e.g., ad hoc function, system, and beta testing). Many developers are amazed at how helpful other employees are when they are approached in the following manner: "You are an expert in testability and reliability and we need your expertise. Will you help review the **newfoo** function for our product?"

Always have the author incorporate review feedback into the functional design specification. Make sure to incorporate reviewer feedback in the form of comments in source code during a code review.

## 7.16 Behind-the-Back Code Reviews

You should perform code reviews (walkthroughs or formal inspections) on all critical source code (you can use a formal or informal approach). The informal approach is less intimidating for developers who are new to the process. The informal approach is based on having peers review each other's workproducts without a formal meeting and documentation. This way, the developer does not have the feeling that someone is looking over his or her shoulder. The disadvantage to the behind-the-back approach is that the engineer's code or specification is not self-checked as closely. When accountability (a review) is lacking, less pride of ownership results (and poor-quality products).

## 7.17 Memory Analysis Tools

Memory analysis tools such as Purify are also useful prior to a code review [WILS95]. Static analysis tools such as **lint** greatly improve the quality of the code and the review by eliminating distracting errors in the code. Better yet, use a tool like INSURE++ from ***ParaSoft*** Corporation. INSURE++ performs static analysis of source code to determine many potential faults (e.g., bad parameters passed to a function and array assignment errors—to name a few). A "zero errors" memory analysis report using all comprehensive functional tests greatly increases confidence in the program. Performing static analysis before testing increases code confidence even more. Memory management analysis products are undoubtedly one of the single most productivity-enhancing tools available today. A significant amount of rework is saved, since a host of bugs are discovered up front, not at the end of the process (or by the customer).

## 7.18 Structural Test Coverage

Statement-level test coverage is extremely helpful prior to the code review (e.g., tools, such as **tcov**, are available on SunOS UNIX systems). Many structural test coverage tools exist today to improve test coverage [WILS95]. Using these tools, project teams are able to achieve an average statement-level test coverage score of over 75 percent. Having automated tests which are designed and developed early in the development cycle greatly improves the overall quality of the product. Remember, test design is always best when initiated during the requirements definition, not after final product integration. Who says you cannot test quality into the product—you can when tests are developed from the start. Planning for the design and development of tests helps the project team to move forward at a steady pace without sacrificing the stability of the product.

## 7.19 Code Review Project Team Goals

One successful method which is used for initiating code reviews is to identify key developers within the company to bootstrap the process of reviews.

These developers are chosen to create guidelines for conducting code reviews and champion the cause (cultivate a best practice). This process can include the following steps:

1.  Form a task force to define the code review team goals, objectives, and time frame. Once the management team has sanctioned the code review team and its goals, focus on the following issues:

    *   What are code reviews intended to accomplish, and why?
    *   How do code reviews benefit the company as a whole? Also, how do code reviews benefit individual groups?
    *   Do not try to reinvent the wheel. (Reuse existing successful methods and approaches, both inside and outside the company.)
    *   Produce a specific guideline. Do not propose a grandiose and generic policy and procedure document (this guarantees shelf-ware which is never used by anyone in the company).
    *   The code review guideline task force is a surgical-strike attack group. Get started, have specific goals, and act quickly. Reviews are more successful when they do not become a career project or a forum for academic debate between project team members.
    *   Having a review process is almost always better than nothing at all. Start with a simple checklist and allow it to evolve into a template, guideline, and then corporate standard (when possible).
    *   Keep track of what worked and what did not work as part of the review process. Make sure to apply each lesson to the code review guideline and standards document.

2.  Investigate "best of breed" code review practices already in progress and gather all relevant information from inside and outside the company.
3.  Define and document the code review guidelines for the company.
4.  Improve the code review guidelines by applying them to as many pilot code reviews as possible (e.g., three to five reviews are a recommended minimum).
5.  Next, release the code review guidelines to R&D management for implementation of code reviews on the next major product release.
6.  Finally, review and reward the team (if appropriate).

## 7.20 Investigate "Best of Breed" Practices

Existing "best of breed" practices are examined by the code review team to obtain a measure of existing and already working code review practices. Next, the code review team must convert the code review outline or checklist into a set of guidelines. This is accomplished by referencing and articulating existing documentation using a procedure-based format. Have an outside consultant review the team's guidelines for the following:

- Constructively critique the code review guideline for general content relative to the ISO9000 standard. See the *IEEE Software Engineering Standards Collection* in the Reference section for details.
- Comment on the code review guideline for specific content relative to the IEEE 1024 documentation.
- Keep the team focused in the direction of International Standards Organization (ISO) compliance. This means that a software engineering handbook of standard policies and procedures is developed and followed by all project teams.

## 7.21 Preliminary Management Presentation and Pilot Reviews

Next, the code review guidelines are prepared for preliminary presentation to executive management. Pilot programs of the guidelines are conducted to validate the process described in the code review guidelines and checklist. After each pilot code review, a post-mortem is conducted to include required changes, additional information, and recommendations for integration with existing code review guidelines.

## 7.22 When to Perform Code Reviews

Code reviews are best when they are performed at every phase of the R&D implementation life cycle (primarily source code development). Any review of a section of code, or code idea, provides an opportunity for additional code credibility (increased reliability and integrity). Although the design and implementation phases are the most crucial opportunities for code reviews, all of the following phases are considered by best practice teams.

### Concept Phase

This phase includes input to the requirements review of the functional specification documentation. *NOTE*: Ambiguity reviews of this work product are very important. See the Appendix on Ambiguity Reviews for further details.

### Requirement Phase

This phase includes input to the design review and documentation; however, feasibility studies, code structures, initial development, and ideas are assessed during code review.

### Design Phase

This phase includes design reviews for every aspect and module. Specifically in the design phase, reviews are applied to the following tasks:

- Functional specification(s)
- Architecture specification(s)
- Design specification(s)
- Code development
- Unit and integration test plans (the earlier the better)
- Expert user training and testing

### Implementation Phase

This phase includes code reviews for every important aspect of each module in the product (i.e., user interface implementation and functionality). You should also consider including usability testing and operational flows, from a users perspective, and adherence to user interface standards:

- Unit and integration test design and development
- Review documentation and training material

### Test Phase

Although the design is generally complete at this phase, feedback from testability, QA, alpha, beta, and acceptance test partners is used to drive additional code reviews for high- risk source code files.

### Installation Phase

Code changes associated with porting to various platforms (hardware, operating systems, graphical interface packages) benefit from the use of code reviews.

### Support Phase

Additional customer requirements and enhancements are enumerated through the problem change request system, and code reviews are applied to the implementation and testing cycles.

# 7.23 High-Level Code Review Checklist

### Pre-Code Review: Meet Prerequisites

[ ] The author has finished coding (is ready for feedback)

[ ] The author has prepared presentation material and is ready to present code and material to the team

[ ] The objective, contents, and scope (product and solution flow) for the review is identified and defined

[ ] The team is identified and roles and responsibilities are assigned

[ ] A code review meeting is scheduled (date, time, place)

[ ] The material (source, header file, tests, and documentation) are distributed

[ ] Participants complete their review of the material and prepare a list of issues and questions for the discussion period

### During Code Review: Process to follow

The moderator is responsible for running the meeting. This person must complete the following tasks:

[ ] Welcome all participants to the code review

[ ] Introduce each reviewer and his or her role in the review discussion

[ ] Outline the rules of engagement and control the meeting (i.e., focus on the product/process/method and not the person)

[ ] Present an overview of the software element for review (be careful with this item, as this can result in a pre-launch of the review)

[ ] Describe the standards, coding practices, and guidelines the team will use throughout the review

[ ] The moderator, author, and reviewers walk through the code in detail. All participants ask questions and raise issues:

[ ] The recorder writes down all appropriate comments and suggestions

[ ] When the review is complete, the recorder or moderator prioritizes the list (with the team) and reviews each action item

[ ] The moderator makes the decision for an additional meeting to review changes (if necessary)

### After the Code Review

[ ] The moderator issues a code review report

[ ] The author archives the code review report with the rest of the material contained in the project file

## 7.24 Detailed Code Review Checklist

### Pre-Code Review

It is important to ensure that you are able to achieve the pre-review prerequisites. This task is usually performed by the author, moderator, or both. It is important to clearly define the objectives of the review. In other words, ensure that the team looks at code in terms of the context required for success (e.g., relevant environment and infrastructure). Other workproducts considered for review include:

- Tools, utilities, and databases
- Usage, work flow, and methodology
- User interface and documentation (tutorials, on-line, help, and reference guides)

Next, you must determine the software element for review (i.e., from the source code interface downward—top-down, bottom-up, or sandwich approach).

- Code prototype
- Data structures
- Algorithms
- Coding plan
- Early implementation

Describe the code or functionality using one or more of the following:

- Design description
- User requirements, use-model, and storyboards (post-it® notes and cards)
- Unit, integration, system, and regression tests

Another important criteria for the pre-code review section is to determine which guidelines to use to verify the source code:

- Coding standards and practices
- Documentation guidelines
- Usability guidelines
- Quality and testability guidelines
- Porting standards

If possible, during the design review, develop a schedule for the code review:

- Milestones and phases for the review
- Inter- and intra-dependencies for the review

## 7.25 Identify Team

Next, the author, project team leader, or both must identify the members of the code review team. This process includes choosing team members according to the type of code and specific expertise required (architect, UI, algorithms, and standards). The author or project team leader must also assign roles by identifying specialists for specific areas of focus (i.e., usability, standards, QA, and performance). Role assignment is performed as follows:

- A moderator is selected by the developer (this is required).
- The developer is not the moderator.
- The moderator helps the developer select reviewers (three to five recommended).
- The moderator also determines preparation time and meeting length (with help from the author).

- It is suggested that the moderator act as a full-time participant (i.e., prepares and reviews the code and all associated workproducts).
- The moderator is responsible for running the review meeting. This means that they are responsible for keeping the meeting focused (i.e., writing down side issues and moving the meeting forward). The moderator is also responsible for helping reviewers focus on review guidelines and not wandering off into black holes.

The moderator must follow up with action item owners after the meeting and assign a timekeeper; otherwise, the action item owners are responsible for keeping track of time. The moderator must oversee the following:

- A recorder is selected for the team. This is strongly suggested. The recorder may also be the moderator or a reviewer.
- The author is required and must be fully engaged in the review process; otherwise, the review is destined to fail.
- At least one reviewer is required; otherwise, you do not have a review.
- Reviewers who are consumers of the workproduct are invited to the review. This is highly recommended for architectural or top-down reviews for understanding.
- Other team members who are suggested to attend the code review discussion include:
    - QA, training, consulting services, and marketing.
    - Other company divisions, or subsidiaries (when needed).
    - Other individuals with specific technical experience (i.e., gurus and specialists).
    - Management (i.e., the author's manager is strongly advised not to attend, unless requested by the author).
    - The product team leader is the most accountable owner and therefore may act in one of the preceding roles; however, project leaders do not always make the best moderators, reviewers, or recorders.

## 7.26  Prepare Checklist

The moderator or project team leader must prepare a checklist for the code review. This checklist includes the following:

1. An outline of what is provided for review.
2. How the review team verifies that the code meets:
    a. Functionality defined by the product reference documentation.
    b. Maintainability defined by the coding guidelines.
    c. Data structures or algorithms for implementation, efficiency, supportability, according to standards.

    d. Code structure modularity, interfaces, black box IO, according to standards.

    e. User interface according to usability standards and guidelines.

## 7.27 Plan Meeting

This critical task is performed by the moderator or project team leader. The following detailed tasks are included in the plan meeting section of the code review:

    a. Distribute review material (the earlier the better).

    b. Schedule the meeting in advance and limit the meeting to no more than two hours. (After two hours of intense discussion and examination, most people are exhausted.)

    c. Review and prepare a detailed list of issues and questions.

## 7.28 Introduction to the Code Review

The introduction portion of the review is performed by the moderator; since this is a difficult session, examples are provided below as guidelines.

1. The moderator welcomes all attendees to the code review meeting. For example, "Welcome to the third code review meeting of the **newfoo** portion of the ABC product."

2. The purpose of the meeting is then stated. For example, "The purpose of this meeting is to constructively (professionally) review the changes that were made to the ABC product's **foobar** access routines. These changes were a result of our last code review meeting on January 1, 1995."

3. The code review team is then identified and their specific roles are stated; for example, "My name is Andy. I am the moderator of this review. My role is to maintain the focus of this review, so that an efficient, constructive and successful discussion is completed. I will interrupt people and redirect the tone and process of the meeting, as necessary, to complete the review on time. The rules of engagement are as follows..." Next, the moderator continues to introduce other team members as follows:

"This is Bill. He is the project leader for the code we are going to review. Bill addresses all the global interoperability issues between the code being reviewed and all other dependent functionality."

"Chris is the author and inventor of the code we are reviewing today. He will address all aspects of this workproduct's functionality."

"Dave is the recorder for this code review. He writes down all issues related to the code review. If an issue is not understood, or recorded to his satisfaction, he may stop the meeting for further review of a particular subject."

## 7.29  The Code Review

During the code review the following tasks are performed by the moderator, project team leader, or author:

- They provide an overview of the section of code for review (as needed, depending on the information required by the team).
- The leader explains the code structure (where each element fits into the bigger picture).
- The project leader explains the design algorithms and methods used by the code.
- Next, they explain the data structures (use of a data structure template is recommended).
- The project leader also lists the applicable standards documents.
- Finally, the project leader explains the coding style employed by the author and team.

## 7.30  Walk Through The Module

The moderator is responsible for facilitating the review based on the guidelines determined by the team. The following guidelines are recommended to ensure a productive meeting (workproduct review):

- Everyone is prepared to participate in the review. Make sure to provide all required information prior to the review, so that the team is ready.
- Always review the product, never the person (author or developer).
- Everyone must always stay professional, no one gets personal. (The enemy is the competition, never your team member).
- Reviewers are not invited to attack the author or other reviews. (Being selected as a reviewer is an honor and privilege, never a right). Train and treasure good reviewers, they are worth their weight in gold!
- The developer is not expected to have to defend his or her code or product.
- The moderator must always keep the discussion focused for a successful and effective review.
- Make sure to get all issues out on the table before any long discussions occur.
- Do not allow the team to waste precious time on issues that are not central to the review.

If the majority of the reviewers are not interested in a topic or issue, or all the correct people are not present for the discussion, write it down and take it off-line. Also, the developer should understand all of the issues raised; otherwise the meeting should be rescheduled. The recorder must record all raised issues, actions, and suggestions.

The following details help facilitate the process of walking through a code fragment or procedure:

- Everyone is introduced by the moderator (e.g., name and area of speciality).
- Next, the purpose of attending the review is discussed (i.e., the role of the code review and any special interests).
- The moderator sets the general criteria and reiterates the general motivation behind the purpose of the code review.
- The moderator briefly presents guidelines and general rules of conduct:
- Make sure to review the code element, never the person.
- Always get all important issues on the table before long discussions evolve.
- Make sure all project team members understand the issues completely.
- All items are taken off-line (as needed) for further discussion.

### The author must set and follow the following specific criteria

- Overview (set the stage and the context for the review).
- Include the background and history of the code.
- Describe the current state of the code (and design if necessary).
- Make sure to include the overall functionality (mapping and interactions).
- Make sure to include any other relevant information for discussion.
- Step through each item contained in the review checklist.
- Review the checklist for functionality, spelling, logic, and other critical factors for success associated with the workproduct.
- Make sure that the team uses a focus checklist, as recommended by the author. This checklist identifies modules and critical functions with high priority.

### Walk through the Code With the Author

- Pick one module or function for discussion (keep it focused).
- Review all input and output, data structures, variables, externals, dependencies, methods, objects, classes, abstract data types, and any other critical components.
- Review the code using a line-by-line or paragraph-by-paragraph method (whichever is best suited for "chunking" the code. The goal is code comprehension).
- Discuss all issues and make sure to record all action items (do not forget to

assign an owner and a completion date).
- Record issues and mark code (make sure to use beacons to help track progress and focus the discussion). Beacons are commonly used to block code into sections and phrases.
- When the module is complete, step through the checklist to the next item.

### Summary

- Discuss and review all findings.
- Create a summary report.

### Record Comments

This task is performed by the recorder. The recorder writes down the problems, actions, and suggestions relating to the following categories or issues for a software module:

### Logic Issues

These issues concern doing the right thing, but incorrectly (e.g., wrong content). Some categorization schemes consider whether functionality is "missing", "extra", or "wrong." Logic usually refers to providing the "wrong" functionality. Functionality usually refers to "missing," or "extra" functionality. Logic therefore refers to something that is logically incorrect (i.e., a defect in procedural, algorithmic, or control logic). Source code is analyzed almost as if it were stand-alone, or without any supporting routines during a code review.

### Functionality Issues

These issues deal with doing either too much or too little (i.e., missing or extra content). Functionality is the category to use when, even if the code is logically correct on its own, it does not correctly map to the functional requirements. This category is used when the code implements too little or too much of the functional requirements. *NOTE*: You may wonder why anyone would care about "extra" functionality. In a very disciplined process, this functionality does not meet the requirements, since no requirement for this functionality exists. Also, it requires additional testing (i.e., resources which are not allocated). Extra functionality may disturb existing functional code which interacts with this "extra" code, since the dependent code may make incorrect assumptions.

### Interface Issues

These problems deal with module interdependency or interface errors. This generally refers to defects in the interface to a routine, for example, inconsistencies with the requirements or design documentation. This also refers to instances when the interface does not provide what other dependent routines assume (require).

### Data Issues

These problems are based on incorrect internal data usage. This category of problems is the most deadly and yet difficult to identify, for example, when data is used incorrectly by a consumer function, or when a provider changes the interface. Both conditions result in either the wrong data type or variable usage.

### Performance Issues

These issues deal with execution speed, memory, and other system resources (hardware and software). Errors in the classification are the result of code which should be enhanced to use less memory or other system resources and to provide better performance results (i.e., wall clock or CPU time). Just as with the other categories, it is frequently up to the owner of the code to determine after the review whether the issue raised is correct (i.e., does performance really need to be improved in this section?). Performance errors include problems which are difficult to determine due to a limited amount of data, for example, whether it is worth changing an interface or data structure (i.e., what is the risk associated with changing the code vs. the risk of not changing it?). Use of performance monitors, profile tools (i.e., **gprof**, **hprof**) and other tools help answer these questions.

### Standards and Nonconformance Issues

These issues deal with coding and internationalization standards. This category is used when the team or the company has standards that the code does not meet, for example, the team's coding standards, company-wide library standards, and internationalization standards. Also included are standards from bodies such as ISO, ANSI, or IEEE.

### Maintainability Issues

Problems associated with the source code are another category. You and the team must understand the code, both now and later. One general rule of thumb is: "If a novice cannot understand it, it is an issue"; however, even if a novice can understand the code, that does not necessarily mean that the next engineer who maintains the code and reads it a year later is able to understand the code. Maintainability includes not only detecting issues related to how the code works now, but also the future (i.e., is it difficult to support and enhance). If the code is not maintainable (some people prefer the term *extensible*), it is usually extremely hard to track down why the failure occurred in the first place.

Be careful of limitations and constraints which are overly restrictive (for example, limits which meet the current requirements, but not foreseeable future desires). As another example, the following statement assumes traditional restrictions on a line of data, but may not be valid in many contexts:

if (number of input chars < 81)

### Documentation Issues (Source Code)

This classification is useful for identifying incorrect or missing documentation. Although there is some overlap between documentation and maintainability, the two workproducts are distinguished. For example, if code is ambiguous and there are no comments to explain it, maintainability is used as a failure category. If standard documentation such as file header information or a description of the function is missing, documentation is usually the best category.

### Other Issues (Source Code)

This category is useful for anything else. The recorder must write down all issues, actions, and suggestions related to the following categories for documentation:

- Not specific enough, more detail is required.
- Too specific for this document, include more information in the lower-level document.
- Missing content, more information is required to complete the review.
- Outside the scope of this document, remove all extra content (source code).
- Not correct (e.g., a statement is in error).
- Ambiguous statement which must be clarified.
- Inconsistency within the document.
- Inconsistency with source and/or supporting documentation.

- An open issue includes an action that needs to be addressed (with an owner).
- Needs to be documented (e.g., this point might be missed if it is not properly highlighted).
- Requirements changed (document does not reflect the functional or product requirements).
- Standards are violated.
- An alternative approach is suggested (e.g., the wording, syntax, spelling, and grammar is recommended for change).

### Review Action Items

The following tasks are performed by the moderator as part of the review process:

- Allow time in every meeting to review the action items.
- Be sure everyone agrees and has a completion date which is assigned. The date in MMDDYY format followed by a sequential number is one method that is useful for assigning a key to an action item.

### End Meeting

The moderator must make the decision to hold another meeting in the future when necessary. The moderator should thank all participants for a productive, constructive, and on-time meeting (if appropriate).

## 7.31 Post-Code Review

The recorder is responsible for generating a report. This report includes the following:

- The team members present at the review.
- The software element reviewed, objective, or overview or both.
- The action items and owners identified during the review.
- The action plan to address all action items.
- The history of each action item and resolution.
- All collectible metrics (e.g., number and class of action items). This is critical. How can you have high-impact reviews and inspections unless results are collected and used to improve the process?
- Communicate to upper management through a management review meeting. Details from the review are never communicated to management (i.e., identifying the engineer's review results discourages management from being willing to have its code reviewed again).

- Include the estimated total preparation and meeting time for the review. This is another critical metric which is useful for evaluating success and improving the review process. Make sure to train and treasure key review team members. They are worth their weight in gold!
- Deliver the report to the team.

### Follow-Up on Action Items

The following tasks are performed by the moderator or project team leader as part of the follow-up process.

- All team members get copies of the reports.
- The owner addresses issues and problems:
  - Fixes defects.
  - Resolves issues.
  - Files problem reports.
  - Enhances the design.
  - Explicitly decides to table an item (open issue).
- Other action owners work on their actions.
- The team addresses broader-scope issues.
- The moderator follows up on action items to ensure that each issue is explicitly considered.
- The moderator also follows up with all action item owners to ensure that each item is addressed.
- The moderator tracks team data and ensures that the road ahead is clear for success.
- The author thanks the review team (also the project leader) for helping produce a better product.

### Examine Action Item Completeness

The moderator or project team leader examines the action item list for completeness.

### Archive Report

The following tasks are performed by the recorder:

- File the action item and action plan report in a designated archive path.
- File metrics report data in a designated archive path (disk location).

# 7.32 Review Guideline Example

### Documentation Distribution

The document is written according to the standards and guidelines provided. If possible, documents are distributed with line numbers, such that all defects are easily referenced. Send guidelines to the inspectors, such as:

- Ignore spelling mistakes (spell check is always performed first anyway). A word may pass the spell check but be the wrong word. Also, consider a grammar check.
- Focus the review on algorithms and suggest improvements with greatest possible ROI.
- Send feedback in a standard defect log format (use the same problem tracking system used for production-related problems—customer problems).
- Classify defects according to the problem tracking systems severity scheme.

### Sending Review Result Data

There should be a guideline that is used by all reviewers and inspectors while filing defect logs. This guideline helps to ensure consistency and adherence to the same standard by the entire team. This method also helps to improve tracking and statistics generation automatically. It should have a header section which describes the following:

- Document Name
- Project Name
- Author
- Reviewer's Name
- Document Version
- Review Date

The review feedback form should contain the following:

- Defect Location
- Defect Category
- Failure Description (Line/Page Number)

## 7.33 Code Review Guidelines

1. Does the code conform to the detailed design?
2. Does the code implement each algorithm correctly?
3. Does the routine name describe what it does?
4. Are the routines modular and easily maintainable?
5. Are well-named "typedefs" or "enumerated types" used?
6. Are named constants used rather than numbers or strings?
7. Is the code well documented (readable)?
8. Is there enough defensive check?
9. Does the code conform to coding guidelines?
10. Is it well indented?
11. Are there too many global variables? Can they be minimized?
12. Is the naming guideline followed consistently while naming a function, variable, global, constant, etc.?
13. Is there any obvious memory leakage?
14. Is the porting guideline followed while coding, especially the use of system calls etc.?
15. Look for performance enhancements in terms of memory or speed. For example, if a common expression is used many times, it is evaluated once and saved in a temporary variable.
16. Is the code written in terms of problem domain rather than implementation domain?
17. Let the compiler check for syntax errors. Let **lint** catch **lint** errors and humans detect human errors.

## 7.34 Questions

1. Why are reviews not as robust or rigorous as inspections for source code?

2. What is the purpose of a code review checklist?

3. Why should you want to perform team building as part of a structured review?

4. What type of technical experts should you invite to a review?

5. Why is it important to have the author select the moderator?

6. Why is management support of a review important?

7. Why do design reviews provide greater return on investment potential

than code reviews?

8. What are some of the responsibilities of a moderator?

9. What are the responsibilities of a reviewer?

10. Why should the author not act as the recorder?

11. Why should the author's manager not attend the review (unless requested by the author)?

12. What is the benefit of having a task force establish code reviews as a new process in the organization?

13. List some of the different types of issues that are classified during a review.

14. Why is it important to classify and record issues encountered during the code review process?

# Object-Oriented Programming (Software Standards)

# 8

O bject-oriented programming is one of the biggest things to hit the software development and user communities during the last few years. There are now a plethora of C++ compilers available on everything from super-computers to laptop PCs. Object-oriented programming is considered to have one of the biggest impacts when it comes to improving software quality (why has it not happened?). Using structured design or modular methods was once believed to be the best method of developing software. However, objected-oriented programming has built on some of the same principles for an even greater return on investment (i.e., data abstraction, encapsulation, inheritance, and polymorphism) [RUMB91]. C++ may be used for object-oriented programming, however, just using this new language does not guarantee an object-oriented program. In fact, many C++ programmers are still using structured design methods, or no design methods at all. This chapter discusses best practices associated with object-oriented (and structured) programming environments.

Leadership, vision, and passion are equally important in the object-oriented programming environment. This is because interface complexity increases dramatically as a result of object-oriented class reuse (lower testability). In other words, in object-oriented development many potential uses (instances) of an object are provided as classes. Therefore, more test design and development is also planned and conducted as a result.

I must admit, the title of this chapter is somewhat deceiving. The real focus in this chapter is on software coding standards. However, many of the principles discussed are mandatory for the object-oriented programming environment.

## 8.1 Foundation Class Libraries

Object-oriented programs are built by using a set of class libraries. These class libraries implement functionality that is used to build software programs and applications. Portability, interoperability, and scaleability are all key benefits associated with class libraries (for example, programs designed on and for Microsoft's 32-bit operating systems). Microsoft's class libraries allow programs to run on all the common IBM PC clones. This also includes the latest generation of high-performance workstations which run Windows NT.

## 8.2 Doing Things Right The Right Way

There are always many ways to design and develop a function. However, there are far fewer ways to do it right the first time. It is important to note that you can develop a product using four or five different programming languages, however, this method is always much more difficult than when a single language is used.

If you are going to use the C++ programming language, you must use an object-oriented analysis, design, and development method to obtain the full impact of the language. Again, once you have committed the design to source code, it is very difficult (time consuming) to go back and redesign a product, object, or function. No technology can ever replace humans who use a well-defined methodology (e.g., requirements, design, review, code, and unit test). Until we truly have computers which make software engineers obsolete, humans are still the best authors of software programs. However, humans also need to use best practices (for example, assertions in source code to make the product more testable). See the chapter on assertions for more details.

Using an object-oriented approach means that you must start thinking in terms of objects (e.g., brake pedal, steering wheel, and turn signal), not just functions—stop, go, and turn. When objects are properly defined and designed from the start, packaging (encapsulation) of software has much more leverage (i.e., more reuse, potentially fewer faults, and better performance). This is doing things right the right way.

## 8.3 The C++ Language

The C++ programming language is not that hard to learn, especially if you already know the C programming language (especially ANSI-C). In fact, if you really want a good check of your C program, use the C++ compiler to compile your program. You may be amazed at the number of actual and potential problems discovered by the C++ compiler, ones that were never detected by the standard compiler.

The C++ language is usually a good choice for software development and has become a standard development language on the PC (and workstation). Most classified advertisements now require C and C++ programming experience. Perhaps most important is the fact that C++ is just a tool, not a complete solution. Software engineering methodology (e.g., test design, verification, validation, and testability) is still as important to success with C++ as it is with the standard C language. In fact, the C++ language makes program testability even lower (more difficult to test as faults are not as easy to detect) than structured design methods. One example is that with a standard C program you may have a variable x. When variable x is used for multiple purposes (e.g., by other consumer functions for other uses), conflicts occur. This problem is greatly expanded through the use of various C++ facilities (e.g., data abstraction, polymorphism, and operator overloading) [RUMB91]. One example of testability concerns occurs when an invalid instance of a class or object is used through improper inheritance. In this case, product reliability and quality are reduced. Therefore, C++ testability is more problematic than simple variables in a structured C program.

On the other hand, when used correctly, object-oriented programming definitely improves productivity. However, when the facilities of the language are abused, object-oriented programming is a terrible experience for the entire project team. There are no silver bullets when it comes to software engineering, development, test, and integration—just hard work. On the other hand, providing the proper infrastructure for you and your team pays significant dividends throughout the development life cycle. The infrastructure for success includes staffing and support for training, tools, methods, processes, reward systems, and metrics.

## 8.4 The C++ Panacea

The C++ programming language is not a solution for each and every possible problem. More importantly, it is critical to provide standards and rules for solving problems. Consistency is the key. Otherwise, if you have a developer that is having a "good day" today and a "bad day" tomorrow, the end result is two completely different styles. Put standards and conventions around practices that seem rather subjective. This makes the program and development process more objective and less dependent on the developer's mood.

Coding standards are one of the best methods to employ for allowing the team to better integrate their workproducts into a customer solution. Many developers believe that they can code however they please. Individualism may be important for music, art, and theater. However, it is not an ingredient of success for a team activity (software development). At a minimum, the developer and customer must always be involved throughout the development process for success to occur.

## 8.5 Standards and Guidelines

Some developers are opposed to explicit use of parentheses to clearly define operator precedence. However, the end result of not providing parentheses is chaos. Consider the following incorrect macro definition:

#define foo(x)x>0 x: -z

Now consider the following definition which is explicit:

#define foo(x)( ((x)>0) ? (x) : -(x) )

The reason the second definition is more accurate is because the expression foo(y - z) yields the wrong result as follows:

y - z > 0 ? x - z : -y - z

With the parentheses, the correct result is provided as follows, since the expression is treated as a subgroup, not a set of independent variables:

( ( ( y - z ) > 0 ) ? ( y - z) : - (y - z) )

Having well-defined coding standards not only defines when to use parentheses, but many other practices (for example, how to create function headers, indent code, build comments, and much more). Developers usually get upset when they must follow a coding standard. Do not allow your team to feel that they have lost the "artistic" and fun aspects of the job. Most customers never see the source code and could not care less if you used the most obfuscated method possible to make yourself look like a genius. If the program does not work, you should not get paid (unfortunately, this is not the case in many software engineering organizations).

Coding standards not only ensure that the team is developing the product using the same style, but that the product is read and understood by more than the author (i.e., code reviews, moderator, recorder). Good coding standards and guidelines also include documentation, testing, and even the way comments are written.

Project team members can look at a piece of code and understand the work product much easier when it is written according to the standard. Another benefit is that the relation to the design or functional specification is more straightforward with standards-compliant code. In other words, you and everyone on the team now understand what a piece of code is doing much more quickly. Also, you now identify interface problems (usually the most complex of all problems) much more easily, since you know where the nasty problems are located.

Everyone must understand they are building the product as a team, not as individuals creating an abstract painting or composing a baroque musical composition. With abstract paintings and some music, the more abstract or complicated the work, the more it is appreciated. Source code is simply a means to an end; a product for the customer. Consistency, accuracy, and efficiency require skilled craftsmen, with experience, knowledge, and the desire to be the best. These attributes (best practices) are critical for success with object-oriented design and development.

Many developers just tolerate coding standards, guidelines, and reviews. Methods for development may seem like a waste of time to developers at first. However, after a while most individuals begin to see that guidelines and reviews make the entire code development process much easier (especially in the object-oriented programming world). This is because a common style allows everyone to understand everyone else's code both better and sooner. One primary goal of object-oriented programming is localization of functions, data, and objects. An equally important goal is building the product the right way the first time. Both goals are impossible without coding standards.

Start implementing standards by using the buddy system. This system is used when peers swap code and informally make comments. Next, move to a somewhat more formal approach where a review is scheduled after select team members have had a chance to examine the code, each with a specific purpose. After a while, most project team members hopefully get comfortable with the review process. Success occurs when standards are simply viewed as a different (better) way of developing code, not unnecessary red tape.

In order to get developers to believe in coding standards and guidelines, they must believe in the standard, and feel a sense of ownership toward the standard. Successful (useful) documented standards are never viewed as a specific individual's coding standard. Instead, the guidelines are viewed as a collection or conglomeration of best practices documented to achieve the greatest possible return on investment.

## 8.6 The Importance of Standards

It is alarming to note that many developers believe that coding standards are not important. After all, standards do not make any direct contribution (i.e., they are not an algorithm, or sexy user interface). Satisfying and delighting customers with products is the goal, not writing the most convoluted or esoteric piece of code no one else can ever understand, compile, maintain, and test.

Good coding standards always go beyond just coding syntax and style. In other words, semantics-related issues are identified and resolved early in the development life cycle (for example, what should and should not be considered an object, or a class). Class and object hierarchy decisions are critical to success; otherwise, a set of objects or classes which are different from an existing set may be created unnecessarily. When everyone on the team performs this unnecessary rework, your objects typically will not work together properly. Now you have risked the entire schedule and project.

Have the project team agree up front what is the best way to write code. Once a standard is decided, this is the new way the group will now write code (an agreement). The standard is usually not the exact way any single individual writes code. The standard is the measure by which the group is expected to code.

The best way to perform object-oriented programming is to use standards and conventions agreed on by the group. Get the team to discuss and fix any problems with the standard and maintain the document with great care. A good indication of trouble if the team has difficulty adopting methods and conventions that it has previously defined is when the standard is useless, or non-functional. This also means that you and the team are wandering away from the team's style of development. Next, you should expect interface and integration problems to occur.

## 8.7 Writing Code The Same Way

Always be realistic and pragmatic about the way software is developed. The key is to have everyone writing code the same way. If an individual with the project team has an object-oriented method that increases the complexity and effort, stop and back up. Always ask the following two questions: "Is this function written as an enabler for our consumers? Will this function increase productivity the way it is written?" If the answer to either question is no, it really does not matter how clean and esthetically pleasing the code is, do not check it into the system. Instead back up and start over. You are most likely going down a wrong road!

Focus on architectural issues early in the design and development phases. Look at functions and code that change frequently (hopefully for the better) to determine the hot spots (areas with great risk of failure). You rarely find a function or module that does not change for the better after the team meets to discuss an issue or question. Unfortunately, it is surprising how hard it is to get some people to meet and discuss a complex interface or function. Without training and experience, many developers take offense or become defensive when someone suggests a code review. Pride of ownership is important to individual success. However, learning and growing is vital to project success (i.e., the ability to accept constructive feedback). Remember, everyone on the project team is on the same team. The enemy is not inside of your company's building, the enemy is your competition. These are the people who are going to eat your lunch if you do not do it the same way. Make sure to train and treasure key developers and reviewers, they are worth their weight in gold.

Many times it is not clear how a particular function operates (either from the design documentation or source code). One example is when one function is used that in turn calls several other functions which have nothing to do (directly) with the original feature selected. The developer must explain what is happening during a specific operation during the review, or everyone becomes lost very quickly. To compound the problem, the developer is usually not at your side during a code examination (defect repair). Therefore, you have to dig through the code yourself to resolve an interface or functional failure.

Always strive to determine all operational interfaces during an architecture review. This is especially important in the object-oriented programming environment to increase testability, reliability, interoperability, and code quality.

## 8.8  OOP Readability

OOP improves code readability and increases modularity. When you create a design always look at every single object and ask the question, "Is this exactly what we want?" If the answer is no, continue to look at where the code is missing the target or falling short of your expectations. Objects, or a complete package that is not compliant with the team's standards of excellence, must always be backed out of the master release source code tree. These problems must always be resolved before code is checked into the central integration system.

Even if you are able to complete a set of class libraries and the performance is great, when a complete product or system cannot be implemented, you must start all over. Do not try to make the interfaces fit when the underlying architecture does not support the required interactions. This is the same as trying to build a single-story 5,000-square-foot home on a 4,000-square-foot lot. Do not get depressed when re-engineering working code. Instead, always discover the root cause and look for the long-term advantage gained. Remember that readability, portability, scaleability, performance, and interoperability are just as critical as functionality (for most products).

## 8.9 Conclusions

- If you do not know how a function or interface is going to work with other supplier functions, do not check it into the system. Instead, go and ask your customers (internal and external) what requirements must be satisfied.

- Always maintain the same kind of environment (i.e., interface consistency) by branching out into sub-teams (job rotation and code reviews are highly successful). A key to success in the object-oriented programming environment is finding and maintaining patterns (practices) which lead to success.

- To build a good product, first build an excellent project team. To build an excellent project team, train and treasure world-class project team leaders. The object-oriented programming project leader understands all aspects of team building. Finding those kind of people is really tough. (Good technical superstars do not always make excellent project leaders, as people skills and technical skills are at opposite extremes of the software engineering spectrum.)

- Highly successful project teams and products require everyone to completely understand the task at hand. The focus is on building a great product as a team, not a big ego as an individual. Remember, objects are only reusable when other members of the team cooperate.

- If you have to make major changes to the product at a late date, get management's support and do it. Do not continue to just hope that the problem or need for change will just go away. Get support from the team and management and—just do it!

- Many tough decisions are made in every software project, regardless of the language. The language and development environment do not make the difference, people do. The difference between having a future and only having a history is a result of the project team. The team is always responsible for the creation of the product. The technology simply provides the raw materials (member functions and class libraries) for product development.

- Being a world-class project leader means that you are able to perform tasks somebody else does not like in the short-term, but will thank you for later. For example, making sure that a class, method, or variable is changed to meet the architectural, functional, or design specification.

- You must be creative, strategic, yet tactical to be a successful leader in any endeavor, especially in the object-oriented programming environment.

- Remember, classes are just types and functions are just tasks. Regardless of the design and development methodology (structured vs. object-oriented) used, teamwork (unity) is the key when it comes to object-oriented programming. Having developers write their own objects (which have already been developed) is simply building a slower, larger, less competitive product.

- Use a tool, such as DISCOVER, to allow the team to understand the architectural interdependencies of both data- and control-flow, especially in the object-oriented programming environment.

## 8.10  Questions

1.  Why are coding standards so important to team success?

2.  What is one best practice for C programming that was mentioned in this chapter which is important in both the structured and object-oriented environment?

3.  Provide an example of how thinking in terms of objects is different than thinking in terms of functions.

4.  Explain why testability is sometimes lower (exposing source code faults is more difficult) in the object-oriented environment? What methods and techniques can you use to guard against this concern?

5.  What are some examples of doing things right the right way?

6.  Why is leadership and vision so important, especially in the object-oriented programming environment?

# Assertions (Making Your Source Code Robust)

# *9*

**T**he answer to many code quality problems is the use of assertions. Assertions are one method commonly used for debugging and testing software (source code). Source code assertions are one of the most basic programming constructs, and yet are extremely effective techniques any C, C++, or other language developer can use. Developers can check assumptions during the development life cycle by using source code assertions (i.e., code vs. functional requirement). Putting assertions in your code is like putting a stake in the ground. Assertions provide watch points for code stability, efficiency, and accuracy.

This chapter discusses several best practices associated with source code assertions. Some believe it is risky to leave assertions in shipped code. After all, do we really want the customer to deal with program termination? Of course not. On the other hand, failures which are properly handled are always better than disasters which are unexpected (for example, loss of data, functionality, performance, response, and usability).

## 9.1 Assertions

The fewer the number of potential errors provided by a public function (i.e., an Application Programming Interface (API) or command), the better the code quality. APIs reduce function complexity and the number of required tests, since each assertion defines the scope of the test (regardless of whether it is a public or private API). What does a programming assertion look like in the C programming language? The following example shows one of many potential assertions used to check the result of the UNIX **read** system call:

```
#include <stdio.h>

#include <errno.h>

main()

{

char *buf;

extern int errno;

if ((read(-1, buf, 1) != -1) && (errno == EBADF))

printf("read assert error for EBADF is correct\n");

else

printf("read assert error for EBADF is NOT correct\n");

}
```

The preceding example shows an assertion based on the requirements of the **read** system call UNIX on-line manual page. If **read** does not return a negative one or an error code equal to **EBADF** (bad file descriptor), the else condition is executed. If the return code from the assertion is correct, the following message is displayed:

read assert error for EBADF is correct

Another example of an assertion is possible using a UNIX command (for example, the UNIX **cp** command is used for copying files from a source location to a destination) [WILS_TAM95]. There are three options provided with the Sun Solaris version of the UNIX **cp** command. The following command test assertion uses the "-i" option. This option requires the user to provide a "y" as keyboard input to confirm the copy whenever an existing file would be overwritten during the copy. The following assertion checks condition where the copy is terminated using the letter "n" as input:

cp -i myfile copyfile

cp: overwrite copyfile (y/n)? n

<The file copyfile is not overwritten>

The other assertion for the "-i" option is to confirm the copy, resulting in modification to the existing file (file is overwritten):

cp -i myfile copyfile

cp: overwrite copyfile (y/n)? y

<file is overwritten>

Another common assertion is provided by Graphical User Interface (GUI) objects. One simple example of a GUI assertion is when a button is placed in the off position (first assertion). The next type of assertion occurs when the button is selected and placed in the on position. Therefore, assertions are state conditions. The complexity of software is not due to individual assertions, but interactions and combinations of states (assertions). Use a tool like TestMaster to develop extended finite state machines (assertions with history) to resolve the combinational problem of assertions [WILS95].

## 9.2  Assertions and Exit Points

Developers (and testers for that matter) get hung up with functions which have multiple exit points (i.e., return statements). It really does not matter if the program has many returns, as long as the correct return code is provided back to the calling function so it can determine the exact exit point (failure location). This is the best possible way to handle error conditions anyway.

Assertions provide watch points for product design, development, and unit testing. Source code assertions are also considered a key part of any coding standard or guideline which is adopted by the project team. Assertions are considered key milestones during the design, development, execution, and maintenance phases of the software development life cycle. Assertions provide key metrics for measuring development and test execution success.

## 9.3  Two Common Problems

There are two common problems which occur with most computer software—users either ignore error messages altogether, while others confuse developer errors with user errors. Use assertions for all serious programmer errors. Programmer errors are never ignored by the user (i.e., they are usually the result of a serious problem which must be reported to the software vendor). Make sure all critical failures (assertions) result in program termination, and that prior to program termination an error message is displayed. Usually, an error is displayed after any special clean-up routines are executed. When these simple rules are followed, far fewer customer complaints are received (i.e., my program just hangs, or stops running).

As an example of a trap handler, there are basically two ways to terminate a program during execution (a process) in the UNIX environment using the **kill** command [WILS_TAM95]. The first method does not use any special options to the command (i.e., it uses the default behavior). This approach simply provides a process id as the only argument to the command. With the process id only method, the program can call a special trap handler (assertion) to clean-up prior to shutdown. This method of handling errors is extremely useful for programs performing database read and write operations. On the other hand, programs which are not designed properly (without a trap handler and source code assertions) terminate without proper shutdown leaving unpredictable results.

## 9.4 Improving Error Circumstances

Assertions improve error conditions (for example, unavailable memory or disk) by providing a trail of bread crumbs (audit trail) for the developer to follow after a failure. Less time is required to support other developers' source code when assertions are used. In other words, code readability and maintainability are improved through assertions.

There are at least two situations where assertions are used. The first is when critical interfaces between packages (routines) are developed or maintained by multiple developers. In other words, function comprehension is improved through the use of assertions when unfamiliar routines are used to perform a function.

As an example, before using a simulation library facility to increase code coverage, you must clear the existing simulation table; otherwise, the results of the simulation are unpredictable [WILS95]. The same is true of functional interfaces. (VistaSIM from CenterLine Software, or MCsim from QASE both provide simulation testing capabilities for increasing test coverage of difficult to perform condition, e.g., **malloc** failure.) Therefore, assertions provide continuity between functions and developers. The other common situation where assertions are used is for self-checking functions.

# 9.5 Self-Checking Functions

Writing code using assertions improves product reliability and quality. There are several types of assertions commonly used in source code (for example, assertions which are so serious they only attempt to provide an orderly and proper shutdown). Other assertions are self-checking, or self-correcting. Programs which are self-correcting result in errors not noticed by the user (a recoverable fault, or failure). Always strive to write code that includes assertions which are self-correcting first. If self-correction is not possible, provide an orderly shutdown. An orderly shutdown must include an error message, followed by program termination.

In both successful and unsuccessful cases, a complete infrastructure is required to assist the developer in performing self-checking. This means that a standard set of interfaces (APIs) is provided for assistance. Therefore, correction is implicit in the programming environment as a result of the standard APIs. As an example, when adding a new function or subsystem, connect the new check function with the main checking routine. Now check that the function walks the data structures, touches every field, and checks the integrity of the expected fields with other actual data contained in the structure. Walking a data structure means that each member of the structure is visited once—read or write. When the result of the assertion is true, the condition is acceptable. Next, continue processing; otherwise, an error must be produced and the condition handled if possible (i.e., recovery from the failure is attempted).

# 9.6 The Strong Assert

Assertions are commonly used to check function call arguments passed by the programmer (another program or user input). Source code assertions are also used to verify the order in which the routines are called. One method of capitalizing on the principle of assertions is through the use of strong assertions. Strong assertions print a message to the user's display that describes the execution problem (for example, source for a program which compares two values may use the strong assert as follows):

strongAssert ( value, "Value is incorrect." );

If the contents of the argument value are missing, or the wrong type of data is provided (i.e., equivalence class failures), the program recovers or halts after the assertion [MYER79]. The same results occur with an out-of-bounds value (i.e., the value is above or below the maximum or minimum threshold).

The other application of assertions is when code is written that depends on one or more program states. Assertions are used to verify that a given set of states are valid. This is particularly important if the code is nontrivial (i.e., low testability as a result of interface design complexity).

Assertions are also useful if the program states are non-obvious. In other words, assertions are critical when the consequences of not satisfying a particular program state are severe. They are also critical when failing to satisfy the assumption could cause the program to generate results which are incorrect or undesirable. Both of the preceding conditions are not always obvious, especially without the use of an assertion.

## 9.7 Two Benefits from Assertions

Assertions serve two critical functions. First, they help you quickly find and fix code that is based on invalid assumptions (defect repair and enhancements). This occurs during code development, or later during unit, integration, and regression testing. Assertions also notify you when changes elsewhere in the program (perhaps made years later) result in long-since forgotten assumptions. In other words, assertions notify you when an enhancement or correction disturbs an interface (i.e., function compatibility).

Assertions are an excellent way to catch source code faults which are not found by using conventional testing. This is primarily because assertions allow code reviewers to better block or chunk source code. Assertions are like beacons to the trained code reviewer. They help block and partition code like paragraphs partition written text.

Assertions also allow the developer to checkpoint the program during execution. As is the case with unit tests, writing assertions as you write source code requires a minimal time investment. However, including assertions in the product source code pays big dividends. In fact, installing source code assertions speeds up the development process. Assertions make the test and debug cycles much more productive, since watch points and test points are easier to track.

Two types of assertions are commonly used:

1.  Standard assertions are generally quick to check and are not in the main path of the program during execution (assumes a standard use-model is used during testing).

2.  In-line assertions are more expensive, since they are in the main path of

the program. They are called in-line or local assertions, since they are enabled and disabled locally. In-line assertions are generally enabled when working and testing the code, and they are disabled prior to promotion to the central configuration management tree.

It is usually a good idea not to remove assertions from the released version of the product. However, the overhead in terms of both time and space should be negligible, or acceptable by the installed user community. A major benefit associated with leaving assertions in the released product is when an assertion fails at the customer site. The following occurs:

- The assertion failure prevents the product from giving an incorrect answer.
- The message which results from the assertion failure tells the file and line number where the problem occurred. The assertion message notifies the user under what conditions the execution failure occurred. This is sometimes enough information for the customer to determine how to work around the problem without assistance. Assertions also provide enough information to help the developer locate the source code fault (bug).
- The message that results from an assertion failure can request the user to inform the software vendor of the problem. This includes giving the vendor an e-mail address or phone number.

Some people believe assertions should never be shipped in production software. After all, if assertions are present and the code is not extremely reliable, the user might have to suffer through having the software die countless times. There is one serious flaw in this reasoning. If an assertion failure occurs, something bad is going to happen, regardless of whether the assertion is there or not. It is possible that some events are relatively harmless; on the other hand, serious problems (corrupting data, generating incorrect results, and running away) are never handled well silently.

To protect the customer, it is always better to terminate program execution in a controlled fashion after an assertion failure. Continuing to run without informing the user that something is wrong (e.g., corrupt database) never results in a happy and satisfied customer.

## 9.8 Shipping with Assertions

Frankly, if you are afraid to ship your code with assertions enabled, you should probably not ship your code at all! Seriously. No data loss or file corruption must occur (by definition of a critical problem) when your program is killed (intentionally or unintentionally). In fact, killing a program after an assertion failure must prevent the product from giving inaccurate results (by definition).

With programs, such as databases, where killing the program may result in loss of data, assertions are still a good thing. However, assertions just interrupt the program and allow the user to back up the data. Assertions never just simply terminate the program in the middle of processing a request.

Why should you never ship assertions to the customer, especially if the likelihood of their being triggered is minimal? The answer is that if the failure condition (trigger) flagged an obvious way to reproduce the failure, this information is beneficial (critical) to both you (the software provider) and the customer.

Errors of all types are always best when they are handled gracefully. Error-handling is a critical part of the overall source code architecture (for the majority of software applications and systems). Assertions are used to catch programmer errors, not user errors. With well-designed and well-written code, a user is not able to cause a fatal assertion (program failure). This is the goal of writing solid code.

## 9.9 Conclusions

- Error and warning messages communicate user errors and mistakes. They should not communicate programming and interface (architecture) failures.

- Assertions are used discretely to communicate programmer errors (for example, calling a function without the proper argument value or data type).

- Source code assertions clearly communicate the key assumptions a developer makes when writing source code. This includes how each interface is handled.

- Assertions increase source code documentation and comprehension. They also improve program testability, readability, maintainability, reliability, supportability, interoperability, and quality.

- Assertions provide a key ingredient to project and product success. This ingredient is a watch point, or acknowledgment which is available to all calling programs. If there is a communication failure, assertions are always there to help arbitrate the situation.

# 9.10 Questions

1. What is the purpose of an assertion?

2. Explain the purpose of a trap handler.

3. How do assertions increase testability (the ability to observe the program's results during testing)?

4. What is the purpose of a strong assert?

5. Write a test assertion for the UNIX write command.

6. How do assertions improve system reliability (interprocess communication between consumer and supplier functions)?

7. What are advantages and disadvantages of shipping products with assertions?

8. How do assertions differ from user errors and warning messages?

# Best Practices for
# Software Testing

# *10*

**M**any developers and QA engineers test their workproducts through the use approach. Instead, more formal methods are required for successful defect detection and containment (e.g., ambiguity reviews, cause-effect graphing, syntax, domain, loop, transaction-, control-, and data-flow testing) [BEIZ90, BEIZ95, MYER79, WILS95]. All these functional testing techniques provide more measurable success criteria, however, they are perceived as too difficult and costly to implement. This chapter discusses several practical approaches (best practices) for software verification and validation (i.e., testing across the entire development life cycle). The following topics are included:

- Testware philosophy
- Functional and structural test coverage
- Positive, negative, and destructive tests
- Compilers and parallel-port testing
- Test management and configuration management
- Nightly integration and roll-up releases
- Test plans, unit, integration, system, and acceptance tests
- Conclusions

## 10.1 Testware Philosophy

Software developers must work closely with their internal and external customers to successfully determine key product functionality. *Testware* is the software (documentation, tests procedures, data, and environment) that is designed and developed in parallel with the development process. Testware is used to verify and validate product and system conformance to customer requirements.

Testware (test plans, designs, programs, data, and documentation) should be marketed along with the products which are tested. Why? So customers can validate proper operation of the product prior to production-level usage.

Testware is one of the most neglected assets of both software and computer companies. Test software is developed and tested by people who have never been trained in formal test design, development, and execution methods [WILS95]. The result is inferior testware (and products).When companies have the foresight to invest in moderate functional and structural testing to improve their products (and testware) they can package and distribute the testware to customers as a valuable tool.

## 10.2  Functional and Structural Test Coverage

Every source file created and maintained must have a test; otherwise, you never know that the function, product, or system is complete and correct (according to the specification). Tests are also created or updated to reflect source code changes conducted to resolve customer problems (*regression testing*) [BEIZ95, WILS95]. Evaluate the success of a test using both *functional* and *structural test coverage* methods:

- **Functional test coverage** (sometimes called testing in the large [HETZ88]) evaluates the relationship between product features and tests. One modest approach to functional coverage is analyzing the number of independent functions compared (mapped) to the total number of tests. More sophisticated methods include switch-level testing, use-models (task analysis for usability testing), test flows, test generators, and grammars [WILS95].
- **Structural test coverage** (sometimes called testing in the small [HETZ88]) measures how much of the product (source code) is actually tested. This method of coverage analysis (for flow-control), is measured in terms of function calls, call entries and exits, statements (blocks), decisions, and conditions. Structural data-flow testing is an excellent, even more rigorous, method of evaluating source code test coverage, since many failures are attributed to data errors, not control-flow.

Measuring structural test coverage alone is inadequate. Customers purchase solutions, not source code test coverage results. Functional tests drive structural test coverage analysis results that come from memory management, control-flow, and data-flow test technology. Memory management analysis tools provide additional metrics for structural test coverage analysis, as well as debugging (for example, memory leaks and access violations). Unfortunately, many developers only use memory management analysis tools for debugging existing problems (reactive not proactive approach). One best practice for memory analysis is using static checkers (for example, INSURE++ from ParaSoft Corporation) to identify and resolve memory access violations during the compilation cycle). One team used this tool to determine an array assignment that was out of bounds preventing a memory fault during execution of that statement.

Be sure to use basic functional and structural test coverage methods and tools before any product is released for commercial use.

## 10.3  Positive, Negative, and Destructive Tests

Always test for failure (expected and unexpected) as well as success [BEIZ95]. Testing to produce an expected failure is a *positive test* (relationship analysis based on the functional specification—a test assertion) [WILS95]. Positive tests occur when the user performs a function exactly as defined in the user documentation (a command example).

A *negative test* is used to attempt to produce an unexpected result although the failure may not necessarily be destructive or catastrophic [BEIZ95]. One example of a negative test is when a command provides an invalid argument (syntax failure).

A *destructive test* attempts to detect an unexpected failure with critical impact using negative testing techniques. One example of destructive testing is when the system power is terminated and then restored, or when corrupt storage device media is provided for read and write operations.

Negative testing considers strategic inputs as well as conditions outside the normal boundaries, domains, and classes defined in the requirements and design specifications. Use an automatic test generation system during the design phase to develop object models for positive and negative state-transition testing [WILS95]. Also, check all critical test outcomes during positive and negative testing. A *test outcome* includes database updates, screen changes, file permission and ownership access constraints, local and system-wide environment variables, system and CPU performance, and memory consumption—to name just a few.

## 10.4  Compilers and Parallel Port Testing

In the past, many successful developers in the UNIX environment relied on the **lint** utility to perform static checking and analysis of source code. The **lint** utility ensures compliance with various system and language standards for the UNIX environment. Unfortunately, **lint** produces many error and warning messages that are very critical (must be acknowledged and resolved). You can use intelligent filters or extended differencing tools to extract only the most important messages [WILS95]. The same filtering process is used by memory management analysis tools as well.

Static analysis filters can ignore important warning messages (for example, not freeing UNIX file locks). Ignoring these warning messages often results in a product or system failure. Therefore, it is best to use care when applying intelligent output filters to reduce the number of filter table waivers or exceptions as the program moves toward each major project milestone. To better isolate and contain error and warning messages, you can block and partition source code. Consider using a tool such as DISCOVER from Software Emancipation Technologies, Inc. for code partitioning, impact analysis, source browsing, and other source code analysis functions.

Parallel porting is another best practice for system- and platform-related testing. All sources are compiled on a development, or reference platform. Next, when compilation results are complete and successful, other platforms (computer systems) are used for native compilation and test execution. The parallel porting process detects code faults through the use of multiple compilers and operating systems early in the development process, not at the end. Before the parallel porting process is started, use a source checker for symbol references located outside the host environment's Application Binary Interface (ABI) and Application Programming Interface (API) standards [WILS95].

## 10.5  Testing and Configuration Management

I believe that many developers still check-in source code to the product release tree (CM system) without creating or executing any functional tests. Never check-in code without a test just because it contains a one-line change. Make sure to perform a local build in your own private work area with your proposed change. The following tasks are recommended as part of your local integration test process:

- Execute as many functional tests as you have (hopefully at least one for each functional requirement).
- Measure the structural test coverage (branch-level coverage is recom-

mended as a minimum). If possible, evaluate the condition and condition/ decision coverage for high-risk modules during the unit test phase.
- Perform memory management analysis.
- Use static analysis tools for complexity and standards conformance.

Make sure to measure the functional test coverage first (i.e., do you have a test for each functional requirement, including the module you just changed?). Unfortunately, few companies measure structural code coverage (branch coverage is recommended but statement is better than nothing). If your functional or structural coverage has degraded as a result of your code change, warning bells and lights should go off. You have just increased your risk and potential for a new or different failure. Also, consider measuring the testability of the change or addition you just made. Testability analysis is used to determine if the program is likely to hide code faults. PiSCES is a tool from Reliability Software Technology (RST) that is used for this very purpose. The PiSCES tool infects the source code with data and logic mutants to determine if the program can detect and "kill" mutants before propagation [VOAS92 VOAS93]. Source code mutants can effect program output and outcomes and reduce testability and reliability.

## 10.6 Nightly Integration and Roll-up Releases

Perform a nightly local integration of all source code changes whenever possible. When the build process (automated technology) completes successfully, a suite of tests must also be executed. At the conclusion of test execution, have the test driver send electronic mail to you with a general pass or fail status. Do not promote changes to the central integration group without adequate functional and structural test coverage and successful test execution results [WILS95].

The central integration group is responsible for taking local source hierarchies and ensuring that they are rebuilt prior to distribution to manufacturing. Never add a function without adding a suitable test, especially if you are patching a shipping release.

While performing a nightly integration, you should always have working code at your disposal. This is particularly valuable when the team is using an evolutionary development approach (i.e., phased approach with incremental milestones).

Also, consider taking all critical fixes and creating a semi-tested roll-up release. The roll-up release must successfully execute all automated regression tests. If any failures occur, these problems must be resolved immediately by the responsible developer. Once the roll-up release is successful, notify all key customers. Roll-up releases are dedicated to a specific platform, usually the development platform used by the R&D group. Many companies attempt to perform a release roll-up every other month. Customers who cannot accept the risk associated with a patch or critical fix (release change without full regression testing) appreciate the benefits of a roll-up release.

## 10.7 Customer Pre-Test

Many customers pre-test new product releases prior to complete company distribution (internal or external). These pre-tests are required to determine if the new product allows employees to continue present tasks. This type of pre-test condition costs the customer a great deal in time, money, and rework costs. Acceptance tests are an excellent way to reduce customer and vendor overhead (i.e., rework, waste, and duplication of effort). *Customer acceptance* tests are best when they are automated (usually a collection of scripts). Acceptance tests demonstrate to the customer that the new product meets their acceptance criteria.

## 10.8 The Goal of Acceptance Testing

The goal of acceptance testing is to shorten (not increase) the customer release cycle. Acceptance tests must reduce the total amount of time required during the qualification process (customer pre-test). Acceptance tests save money. They also reduce, if not eliminate, many headaches for the customer and you, since the criteria for success (acceptance) are clearly defined in the form of a test suite early in the project life cycle.

## 10.9 The Problem (Requirements)

Most software companies want to provide solutions, however, without careful analysis, the solution (new product) provides more new problems. To have a successful solution, you need to have a good understanding of the customer's requirements. This understanding is based on use-models, data requirements, and the general methodology used. Many developers have little knowledge of how their products are actually used in the real world. This must not be the case.

Product marketing (the product manager) is expected to capture the customer's requirements and convey this information to the development group (engineering). However, development of a successful solution for a complex problem is impossible without direct input from the customer.

Not allowing engineers direct communication with the customer is also difficult on the end-user (for example, companies developing sophisticated products using advanced Electronic Design Automation (EDA) software take from 6 to 12 months to complete a design). The majority of this time is dedicated just to new release qualification (i.e., compatibility and regression testing). This validation process usually requires the customer to verify that a new product release does not disrupt existing design flows (i.e., design use-models and methods). Therefore, direct communication between the customer and the vendor is critical to success.

Have the customer involved in all phases of product development (for example, development of the marketing concept proposal, engineering functional specification, design documentation, and beta testing). Open communication via electronic mail, regular teleconferences, or video-conference meetings are also mandatory to project and product success.

Product success requires a team effort. This effort must include a partnership with key customers. Having multiple customers means that all requests are prioritized and factored against engineering resources. Use a matrix (Quality Function Deployment or QFD) to balance customer requirements with resource capabilities.

## 10.10  Expected Results

The end result of close interaction with the customer is achieving a working solution sooner. This means that the customer does not need to worry about products which do not work together (i.e., interoperability and interface failures). Also, the customer now influences the software development process and therefore obtains good technical support.

## 10.11  Benefits of Acceptance Test

Engineering benefits from acceptance testing by obtaining early feedback from key customers. Early information ensures that only competitive products are developed. Have customers provide acceptance tests early in the development life cycle (during the requirement phase is ideal).

Excellent service and support are also critical to project success (i.e., customers are more engaged with the product when the existing environment is integrated into the plan). Conversely, simply dumping a feature, or system, in the shipping department does not provide a complete solution. Excellent service usually results in higher product sales revenue. Acceptance tests are a "win-win," since the customer's tests are integrated into the regression test suite. This process verifies that product changes do not result in methodology or functionality incompatibility failures as a result of a new product release.

Developers and testers are always more satisfied when they know exactly how their products are used by the customer. Therefore, engineering now designs and develops the right new products from the beginning (i.e., validation is implicit throughout the process, not tested at the end).

Customer acceptance tests reduce the total amount of time to market for both the company and user. This means all test procedures and data are highly leveraged (i.e., excellent functional and structural coverage is provided by the acceptance tests). High leverage also comes from analysis of the control-flow, transaction-flow, and data-flow aspects associated with use-model development and validation. Finally, acceptance tests measure how comprehensive, unambiguous, and correct the product feature set is, prior to final delivery.

## 10.12  Test Plan Best Practices

Test plans are ideal when they focus on content and not just format [WILS95]. This is a common problem with many test plans. Make the requirements and design specifications incorporate testability, test methods, and tools. When possible use a single document for product requirements and test requirements.

Include all specifications and test plans on a web page to ensure that structured (modular) design methods are used for all text (html) documents. Access through a web interface also increases accessibility of information. Finally, partitioning specifications and test plans by subject also increases exposure and review participation. This means that project team members and key customers no longer must wade through several hundred pages of data to find a few critical pages of information detail they wish to review.

Successful plans always lead to automated test design and development. (Make sure the return on investment is justified—consistency, accuracy, and efficiency improvements.)

## 10.13  Unit Test Best Practices

Unit tests are best when they are derived from hidden text contained in the functional specification (test procedures). They must also be good enough to be packaged and distributed. This is implemented by executing test functions (unit tests) as part of the on-line help system.

Problem report test cases are used as input to the unit test development process. (Root cause analysis is an important ingredient to turn this reactive method into a proactive approach to process improvement.)

It is also especially important to include unit test design and development as a vital part of the product development and maintenance schedule. Therefore, unit tests are scheduled as part of the product development life cycle (preferable before code development).

A central test harness is important to unit test success [WILS95]. The harness is used to provide test sharing by the user, customer, engineering, QA, and technical support. The test harness or environment must provide flexibility for Bourne and C shell scripts, PERL, C (and other programming languages) utilities and commands [WILS_TAM95].

Make sure to develop a standard template for unit tests. This helps ensure that only flexible tests are developed. This results in a minimal amount of rework when product functionality changes.

Unit tests are best when they are analyzed using dynamic and static metrics analysis tools to ensure the greatest possible return on investment. (This is also important for integration, system, and acceptance tests.)

Application engineers and field support individuals create or modify unit tests for customer demos. These tests include function and performance tests. You can use these tests as part of the product validation process to leverage this investment. Consider developing a contribution tape release for customers. A *contribution release* contains all other workproducts for validation testing. This package contains various public domain utilities and program sources. There are licensing restrictions, but this is not a problem when copyright rules are followed.

## 10.14  Integration Test Best Practices

Integration tests are best when they are derived from root cause, impact, and risk-based analysis techniques, not a rote process of regression testing. Integration tests (testing all product interfaces) is difficult, especially when all consumer software is not registered with the application. Therefore, the first step to integration testing is to know all function call entry and exit points for the application under test.

Integration tests are best when they are assisted by an automated process (that is, little user intervention is required). Writing integration tests (for example, library test assertions) can be easy when well-defined interfaces are provided. Without well-defined interfaces, integration tests are almost impossible to develop and maintain.

In most cases, intelligent filters are required for baseline comparisons (that is, golden file or expected vs. actual test results). Make sure to include test outcomes, not just output for test comparison. Outcomes include information other than display output (for example, environment variable creation, deletion, and modification). Make sure tests are written using built-in self-checks (assertions), not a single point of failure (usually located at the end of a test). Always check exit, return, error, and file differences, not just that a disaster did not occur after test execution (a touch test) [WILS95].

## 10.15  System Test Best Practices

System tests are more than the accumulation of unit tests. System testing includes use of random seed and use-model test execution of a suite of functional tests (to name just two of many approaches). System testing also includes test execution and analysis using platform-specific attributes. These tests take into account the operating system, compilers, peripherals, networks, and applications used in the test environment.

Platform specific attributes (for example, operating system, compilers, peripherals, networks, and other critical features) are vital to successful system testing. System testing is not the same as integration testing, it is a super-set.

Make sure you always have a reference platform defined before you attempt to perform system testing [WILS95]. This reference computer system acts as the tiebreaker in the event of an incompatible library, utility, or other system environment failure.

Consider using a method of multivariable testing or orthogonal arrays for test set reduction during system testing [WILS95].

## 10.16  Acceptance Test Best Practices

Acceptance tests benefit both the customer and supplier through improved performance, reliability, interoperability, time-to-market, and revenue.

You can set up a validation lab, which is a secure environment used to design, develop, and execute acceptance tests with technology partners (critical customers). This secure lab provides an exact duplicate of the customer's test environment for development and maintenance of acceptance criteria.

Coverage tools are useful for determining acceptance test suite value (that is, function call, block, decision, condition-decision, data, and other structural test coverage metrics) [MYER79].

Documentation examples are always an excellent input source for acceptance tests. Documentation tests are an integral part of the development and execution process.

Engineering benefits from acceptance testing by obtaining early feedback from key customers. Early information ensures only competitive products are developed, not dustware. Have customers provide acceptance tests early in the development life cycle (during the requirement phase is ideal).

Excellent service and support are also critical to project success (that is, customers are more engaged (happy) when the existing environment is integrated into the new product marketing and business plan). Conversely, simply dumping a feature, or system, into the customer's shipping department does not provide a complete solution. Excellent service usually results in higher product sales revenue. Acceptance tests are a "win-win," since the customer's tests are integrated into the regression test suite. This process verifies that product changes do not result in methodology or functionality incompatibility failures as a result of a new product release.

Developers and testers are always more satisfied when they know exactly how their products are used by the customer. Therefore, engineering now designs and develops the right new features from the beginning. This means that validation is now performed throughout the process, not just at the end.

Customer acceptance tests reduce the total amount of time-to-market for both the company and the user. This means all test procedures and data are highly leveraged (that is, excellent functional and structural coverage is provided by customer acceptance tests). High leverage also comes from analysis of the control-flow, transaction-flow, and data-flow aspects of the customer's use-model when acceptance criteria are packaged into a test suite. Finally, acceptance tests measure how comprehensive, unambiguous, and correct the product feature set is, prior to final delivery.

## 10.17 Conclusions

- A successful testing strategy treasures testware while analyzing the functional behaviors (relationships) of all documented functions. This strategy includes testing error and warning conditions by using assertions derived from the functional specification, user documentation, and architectural plans. This strategy is further supplemented by the use of both functional and structural test coverage analysis based on both positive and negative tests. Functional and structural test coverage analysis is performed throughout the development life cycle, not just at the end.

- Successful developers rely on nightly integration cycles (builds) to eliminate the big-bang (late failure) approach to source code and product integration. Another successful best practice includes using a parallel porting process to detect system failures early in the development cycle.

- Successful unit, integration, and system tests are documented, designed, developed, executed, and analyzed using an integrated test management, defect tracking, and source code management system. Software development environments have had this capability for years, why should test environments not have the same?

- Successful developers use tools as part of their personal software process. Many of these tools provide easy methods for improving code quality (for example, **lint**, ANSI-C, **tcov** or PureCoverage, Purify, Quantify, and XRunner) [WILS95].

- System testers also use tools to improve their verification and validation processes. Software test engineers and developers use a tool such as PureVision from Pure Software, Inc. for alpha and beta test management and process improvement. PureVision is used to transmit debug, usage, and reliability information directly from the customer site.

- Successful developers also use tools such as INSURE++ from ParaSoft Corporation for static memory analysis of source code. These individuals also perform source code impact analysis using a tool like DISCOVER from Software Emancipation Technologies. They perform impact analysis to determine what existing code may break as a result of a proposed change.

- Successful projects are carried through by team members who realize that everyone is responsible for quality. Therefore, everyone on the team is involved in the testing process (from the concept phase through product maintenance) [IEEE94].

- See the Appendix for an outline and checklist for verification and validation.

## 10.18 Questions

1.  What is testware and what does it include?

2.  What is the purpose of functional test coverage?

3.  What is the purpose of structural test coverage?

**4.** What is the purpose of a negative test?

**5.** How does a negative test differ from a positive test?

**6.** What is the purpose of an acceptance test?

**7.** What is the purpose of a unit test?

**8.** What is the advantage of a nightly integration vs. a build every couple of months (or even years)?

**9.** Explain the benefit and purpose of a parallel porting process.

**10.** What is the purpose of a static analysis tool?

**11.** What are some of many static analysis methods that can be performed?

**12.** What is the purpose of a central test harness?

**13.** What are some best practices associated with test plans?

**14.** What is the purpose of a reference platform?

**15.** What is the purpose of impact analysis?

# Problem Reporting
# and Tracking

# 11

R&D and QA engineers must cooperate (work together closely) to achieve success. The success of the working relationship is often measured by the contents of the problem reporting and tracking system. This chapter contains best practices associated with a key system used throughout the software development process in any organization—problem reporting and tracking.

## 11.1  Problem Reporting and Tracking Systems

Problem reporting systems and databases provide one of the best and most commonly used methods of communication between customers and vendors. On the other hand, if you are unable to understand a user request or problem report, it is usually best to talk directly over the phone. If both companies provide a teleconference system, that is even better (but more expensive to maintain and operate). Many computer systems now provide teleconferencing directly from a PC or computer workstation. Electronic mail is another excellent means of communication and is the least expensive (less than a phone call).

Regardless of how you contact the customer, first notify the appropriate sales representative and applications support engineer. The field or application engineer is often able to help you answer the question without having to contact the customer. Also, make sure that you clearly understand the problem as reported in the problem report system before recommending a solution. (The English language is by nature often ambiguous, see the appendix on ambiguity reviews for details.) This may sound like a fairly obvious statement, however, many developers and project leaders forget these simple, yet important best practices for customer exchange.

Consider face-to-face meetings with the customer whenever possible to see the actual context for customer usage. Customer visits are especially useful for improving product usability. Using a video camera helps you and the project team to better understand how to improve product usability through task analysis. Another benefit of customer visits is the ability to record customer use-models (product operation) with automated testing technology (e.g., XRunner and FlightRecorder from Mercury Interactive).

Good problem reporting systems provide a single-threaded method of control between multiple users. Users are able to append messages to the original posting and develop a single thread of communication and history. This information stream includes questions, suggestions, and proposed solutions. From this database, key information to resolve critical problems is obtained, either directly by the customer, or though a support representative. Using the problem report database, technical support engineers can determine what files are required to resolve serious customer problems. Make sure to always ask for confirmation from the support engineer or customer before closing a problem report that is marked as fixed.

All project team members must spend time up front before they change one test, page of documentation, or line of source code. It is critical that each team member fully understand the implications, impact, and risk associated with each change. Remember that complexity increases as the number of changes increase. This is even more dramatic when the changes occur within a small time domain.

## 11.2 Timely Information Exchange

An important best practice associated with maintaining customer satisfaction and with winning loyalty is successful information exchange. Every problem report that is submitted by an internal or external customer is always responded to immediately (by best practice teams). This means that even if the response is, "Here is the fix to your problem," you must acknowledge and understand the problem. Alternatively, you might say, "Here are some questions related to your problem." In any case, time is usually of the essence with most problem reports. Therefore, it is critical that you provide a timely response to each and every problem report. Use special keywords to reflect the status of a problem (for example, document, critical, next release). These keywords reflect the proposed solution to a problem and are used by team members for solution agreement.

It is critical that each engineer always update the problem report database the moment a problem appears. The same process holds true for voice mail. Urgent messages are best left using voice mail. These messages require an immediate response. Therefore, engineers who only process voice mail once a day can potentially leave a customer in a serious situation for several hours. Sometimes, the customer may even leave a critical piece of information using the voice mail system which can save hours of unnecessary debugging or trouble-shooting effort. Less critical issues are best handled using electronic or postal (snail) mail.

Never leave an issue open with a customer without determining the next step or course of action (i.e., when to discuss the problem again). Try to always bring closure to all open issues. If you cannot resolve the issue, communicate to the user or customer that you are waiting for some specific details. Also, make sure they understand the problem is now contained in the problem report database. It is important to never leave a customer problem or question dangling, such that the customer or vendor is unable to determine the current status. Customer satisfaction is always the most important part of your job. They (the customers) are the reason you and the company exist.

## 11.3  Problem Report Backlog

Communication is the key to successful customer relationships and end user loyalty. Some company products are known to have a large backlog of problems, usually due to neglect and poor management. It is important to look at each problem in detail and respond directly to the user to reduce the problem backlog. If appropriate, make sure to copy all sales and support individuals involved in dealing with a particular critical customer account. Developers frequently need to ask the customer questions to solve a problem. Therefore, direct customer contact is required to acquire a complete understanding of the problem. After the problem is resolved or responded to, most of the backlog diminishes.

Always strive to get and remain ahead of the number of incoming problem reports. Small problem backlogs are noticed by management as a significant accomplishment and are a basis for reward. Problem report backlog is a critical metric for measuring success along with features and schedule. Product complexity always seems to increase and never decrease. By keeping a small backlog in the problem report database, you and your project team are better positioned to tackle new products, features, or even other projects.

## 11.4 Problem Report Priorities

It is important to use a problem tracking priority system which includes:

- A customer requested priority
- Company priority
- R&D priority

Many times, engineers ignore problems with low severity. Low priority problems often have a simple work-around which does not result in any loss in data, productivity, or efficiency. High severity problems are either show stoppers (e.g., work stoppage, data loss) or serious problems. Show stoppers usually require immediate attention, since no known work-around to the problem exists. Serious problems may have a difficult work-around and therefore are resolved in the next major product release. Ignoring serious or even low-severity problems is very dangerous, especially when low-severity problems are improperly marked by the requestor or support engineer (e.g., when a serious priority problem is marked as a low-severity one and ends up costing the customer millions). If you make an error in judgment, always error in the customer's favor. Always ask the following questions when evaluating a problem report:

- Is there any loss of data as a result of using the function?
- Is there any major loss in functionality using the function?
- Is there a simple work-around to the problem?

If the answer to any of the preceding questions is yes, the problem is resolved immediately (no ifs, ands, or buts).

Regardless of the problem priority, always have the philosophy and mind-set that all problems must be resolved. Better yet, all problems should be prevented. Successful developers and project teams always have the mind-set of despising any bugs that attempt to hide or invade their code, documentation, test suite, marketing proposal, or training material. This attitude must prevail for both enhancement requests as well as serious show-stopper problems.

## 11.5 Quality and Problem Reports

Quality is not just a low number of problem reports or customer complaints. Quality is defect-free, robust, efficient, reliable, easy-to-learn and use products (solutions). High quality is also high-performance products which exceed customer requirements and expectations. Talk about all of these aspects of quality, since if you miss any one item, you and the team have failed. Object-oriented programming improves quality when well-defined methods and process are used.

On the other hand, high-quality object-oriented software does not mean that the customer never needs training and support. Most customers are usually willing to pay for some level of technical support and training (depending on the product). This support includes technical consulting to help train the customer. Training helps the customer to understand how to use the product to the maximum benefit possible (for example, the most efficient way to design a database schema or develop a device driver).

Customers are usually unwilling to pay for support when it means that someone will write (hack) two products together that were not properly designed from the start. After all, most customers normally assume product and function interoperability is available from the beginning. Successful companies market and sell products designed and integrated to work together as a seamless solution.

## 11.6 Conclusions

- Problem reporting and tracking systems are the vehicle from which to perform daily company business (operations).

- Make sure all your engineers and managers are trained in how to use the problem tracking system. This training includes when to use face-to-face conversations instead of electronic communication.

- Project teams must use the problem tracking system to constantly measure and monitor the health of the product (and project team). These teams constantly strive to keep the backlog to a minimum, however, they balance the problem backlog with other critical requests (e.g., critical benchmarks, new sales and maintenance deals, product development, maintaining and improving customer satisfaction and quality).

- There are many problem management and tracking systems [WILS95]. Make sure you and your organization take advantage of this technology.

- The customer is the reason you and your company exist. This is especially important to realize when you must work with the most difficult user on the face of the earth. I do not care how talented a software professional you are, if you cannot work with the customer successfully, you and the company will suffer.

## 11.7 Questions

1. What is the purpose of a problem tracking and management system?

2. What are some techniques for improving customer communication?

3. What are some methods for capturing usability problems?

4. Why should you consider using and integrating these techniques with the problem management and tracking system?

5. What are some potential keywords to use with your problem tracking and management system for communication between team members?

6. Explain the difference between a low and high priority problem report.

7. What is meant by timely information exchange? Why is it important?

# Checklist For Best Practices

**M**any companies are missing out on a very simple, but effective method of conducting process and cultural change. A checklist is one of the best methods available for identifying methods, tools, and processes for success at specific phases of the development life cycle. The following checklist is an outline recommended for customization to match your specific environment and company culture. After the checklist becomes successful, formalize it into a guideline or better yet, a corporate-wide standard.

## A1.1 Product Requirements

Criteria for development and review of product requirements include:

- Ambiguity checks (e.g., cause and effect graphs are developed based on information provided in the product requirements specification)
- Completeness checks against customer requirements
- Accuracy checks (e.g., comparing requirements documentation with concept proposal documents)
- Consistency checks (e.g., formal technical reviews and inspections)
- Problems and limitations with all product functions identified
- Enhancement requests incorporated into document
- Alignment with future direction (i.e., concept proposal and business plan)

## A1.2 Requirements Maintenance

These activities include:

- A complete functional specification is provided and supported
- A working prototype is used to validate a core algorithm
- Core requirements are clearly defined and documented (see Ambiguity Reviews Appendix for testing techniques)

## A1.3 Documentation

Functional specification and design document activities include:

- Basic sanity check of the requirements (complete, accurate, unambiguous, efficient, and effective)
- Identification of dependencies (parent/child relationships)
- Customer review of specifications (this is mandatory)
- Basis for documentation (have the technical writer start early!)
- Documentation maintained (use CM system for version control)

## A1.4 Code Reviews

Best practices for code reviews include reviews conducted throughout the implementation phase, not just after the product has been shipped and returned with many problem reports. Code reviews include the following:

- Earliest start (when code compiles)
- Latest start (beta and acceptance test phases)
- Develop and maintain written standards for group that include:
  - Percent of all code reviewed and other related metrics
  - Number of defects detected per review (log and track)
  - Make sure that reviews are considered useful as a learning tool
  - Successful reviews instill teamwork and team interaction

## A1.5 Software test and QA tools

- Unit code and test
- Functional testing (control-, loop-, data-, and transaction-flow methods)

- Integration testing (threaded, selective, full, call entry/exit, top-down, bottom-up, sandwich, and hybrid methods)
- System and solution testing (acceptance, network, platform, use-model, performance, interoperability, and other final test methods)
- Test coverage (functional, structural, reliability, testability, and other code-based test analysis methods)
- Code reviews (walkthroughs, inspections, buddy system, peer reviews, and other review and analysis techniques of source code)
- Beta test (agreement, automated follow-up, metrics collection, post review and other best practices associated with beta testing (see *UNIX Test Tools and Benchmarks*, Prentice Hall (1995) for further details)

## A1.6  Testing and Quality Tools

- Detailed unit, integration, and system test plan
- Memory management and debugging tools (e.g., testing and debugging using memory access violation and leak detection)
- Strict ANSI-C compliance checkers
- Static structural analysis (e.g., **lint**, testability, complexity, and standards conformance checkers)
- Structural test coverage (testability, complexity, interoperability, safety, reliability, and other code-based dynamic analysis methods)
- Parallel porting (multi-platform build and test in parallel)
- Problem report statistics collection and analysis:
  - Number of incoming critical and important problems
  - Number of outgoing critical and important problems
  - Number of regressions (lost functionality)
  - Change in code complexity vs. defect density
- Considerations for beta testing:
  - Extended beta planned from start
  - Detailed beta plan
  - Committed beta customers (engagement and agreement)
  - Committed to beta customers
  - Turn beta sites into reference accounts

## A1.7  Key Points to The Best Practices Checklist

Spend the time up front to properly collect, prioritize, and review customer requirements. Do not change functional requirements without serious consideration. Always manage all distractions carefully by asking the difficult questions first (e.g., is this a must, should, or could priority?).

Having complete, accurate, and unambiguous specifications simplifies maintaining the requirements in the future. People make code reviews successful. No machine, software, or any other technology can substitute or replace the human thought process and power of synergy during a successful review! Written standards are critical to the establishment of guidelines for reviews, testing, coding, and maintenance. Checklists, guidelines, and standards set everyone's expectations (i.e., a contract is developed vs. an operation using guesswork).

# Beta Test and Customer Acceptance Test Checklist

## B1.1 Introduction

This document is organized according to objectives, ownership, and process. Three phases are associated with successful beta testing. This is followed by a detailed checklist of steps required for successful customer acceptance and beta testing. Each step is identified as either must, should, or could. A must step is highly recommended. A should step is considered very carefully. Finally, a could step is suggested, but is not critical to success. I would like to thank the following individuals for there help in creating the following checklist: Dick Albright, John Murphy, John Perry, Michael Griesbach, Linda Prowse, and many other employees at Cadence Design Systems.

## B1.2 Objectives

- Beta testing is a positive and desirable experience for customers and employees
- Customers must always have a feeling that their investment in beta testing is worthwhile
- New products are introduced using a rigorous process which includes testing in the real customer environment
- Products or features must operate successfully in a customer environment
- A stable and repeatable process is always used for conducting beta tests
- Feedback from testing is used to obtain input for future product

releases

## B1.3 Ownership

The product team must own the process used for beta testing. This is key to product release success. Individual dedicated resources on the team, such as marketing and QA, must own particular parts of the beta test process, especially where their expertise and focus will add significant value.

## B1.4 Three Phases of Beta

1. *Planning and customer engagement phase*. This phase can start when product specification is first created and should end when the software is successfully delivered to the customer for testing.

2. *Execution Phase*. This is an intense period of time that starts when the software is first delivered to the customer for testing. This phase ends when the software reaches an acceptable level of stability according to the beta test objectives or customer acceptance test criteria.

3. *Wrap-up phase*. This phase is dedicated to the collection of summary and evaluation information. This includes feedback and closure on all open issues.

## B1.5 Beta Test Best Practice Checklist

### B 1.5.1    Beta Team Responsibilities and Resource Allocation

[ ] Identify an overall beta test coordinator from project team (Must).

This role is taken on by any member of the product team depending on resources and available skill sets. A dedicated marketing resource may own the customer identification and qualification. A dedicated QA resource may own the resolution of issues between the customer and the R&D team. One person from the product team is identified as the technical support contact for questions received from each beta test customer.

[ ] R&D support budgeted, identified, and available prior to beta test (Must).
[ ] A champion (contact) for each site is identified (Must).
[ ] Responsible parties (point of contact) are identified for both the customer and company prior to the start of beta testing (Must).

[ ] All product and solution features for testing are identified in advance (Must).
[ ] All primary features and functions are identified (Should).
[ ] A matrix of features to tests is created (Should).
[ ] All primary customer uses are identified (Should).

### Site Selection

[ ] Strategic customers are involved in the requirements and design review processes prior to the beta test phase. In general, these customers are excellent candidates for beta test sites (Should).
[ ] Establish a qualification checklist to define good customer candidates (Should).
[ ] Select beta test candidates (Must).
[ ] Sign and complete beta test agreement (Must).
[ ] Functional specification reviewed with customer (Must).
[ ] Non-disclosure documents completed by customer (Could).
[ ] Customer questionnaires completed (Could).

### Project Plan

[ ] Customer feedback and metrics under a control system for weekly review (Must).
[ ] Weekly conference calls are arranged prior to the start of the beta test process (Must).
[ ] The project schedule includes sufficient time for feedback to customer during beta test period (Must).
[ ] The beta test customer provides sufficient breadth of testing. This includes installation, documentation, interoperability, stress, load, performance, and other system test methods (Should).
[ ] The project schedule includes time to resolve and distribute corrections to problems discovered during the beta test period (Should).
[ ] The test data and product use is documented (Should).
[ ] Buy-in across groups such as sales, sales management, field support, marketing, engineering, and tech marketing is provided (Should).
[ ] An e-mail alias is created for feedback and sharing experience by marketing, management, field support, and sales (Could).
[ ] Executive management provides visible support for beta test, especially for new product introduction (e.g., newsletters, etc.) (Could).

## B 1.5.2   Company Beta Test Champion Responsibilities

It is recommended that only one person be assigned for each beta test or customer acceptance test site. The beta test champion is usually a field support engineer. This individual is very familiar with the company products used by the customer, as well as the customer's environment.

[ ] Assist with all beta test problems (Must).

[ ] Document, provide feedback, and report problems using problem management system (Must).

[ ] Forward both new and unresolved feedback and problem reports to the beta project team (Must).

[ ] Beta site support engineers are trained with new product technology prior to the start of beta testing (Should).

[ ] The support engineer assists with loading the software (Should).

[ ] They will file, submit, and record feedback and metrics (Should).

[ ] The field support and sales employees will collect and report (via e-mail alias) how the competition is responding to the new product introduction (Could).

[ ] Support engineer extends an invitation to the company beta customer appreciation day (Could).

### B 1.5.3    Customer Responsibilities

Beta testing is an advantage to both parties (win-win) when strict criteria are used to manage the effort. For example, you must determine what the customer is really interested in using prior to beta testing.

[ ] A customer letter and agreement is received to test the features that the company needs tested. This is in the context of the customer's environment (Must). Note: This agreement is provided to ensure the success of the beta test process.

[ ] The schedule and resources available for beta testing are committed (Must).

[ ] Customer management support is in place for beta testing (Must).

[ ] The beta test process is presented and viewed as a collaboration with the company (a partnership) (Should).

[ ] The customer agrees to act as a reference account at the end of the beta test period (Could).

[ ] The customer will test in a real-life situation or environment, not as a simple evaluation or demonstration (Could).

Beta testing is best when it is not performed in a mission-critical or with a product that is already in the critical-path for production release. The risks are too great and the customer is not able to provide adequate attention to the process associated with beta testing.

# B1.6 Execution Phase: Company Beta Team Responsibilities

[ ] A release mechanism is in place from the start of the beta test to provide timely updates to customer (Must).

[ ] Weekly telephone conference calls are scheduled (Must).

[ ] Feedback and metrics are reviewed weekly (Must).

[ ] Beta site field support personnel are trained with new technology prior to the start of beta testing (Should).

[ ] Customer data and usage (processes) are preserved for regression testing (Should).

## B 1.6.1    Wrap-up Phase: Company Beta Team Responsibilities

[ ] A post-review process (post-mortem) is conducted after the beta test process (Should).

[ ] An improvement plan is constructed for the next beta program (Should).

[ ] A "What worked and what didn't work" list is created (Should).

[ ] A beta customer day is scheduled (customer and project team meet). This includes final comments on product and beta process (Could).

# Ambiguity Reviews

## C1.1 Introduction

The English language provides many potential pitfalls when used as a basis for defining product requirements (i.e., what the product does). This same fact applies to how detail designs are written to describe the operation of a feature, product, or system. There are many potential areas of ambiguity as a result of using the English language. This appendix contains several best practices for reducing ambiguity of almost any workproduct (e.g., requirements, design, source code, tests, training material, and other critical components associated with the delivery of software solutions).

I would like to thank Richard Bender of Bender & Associates for his pioneering work in this area and for allowing me to use much of his material concerning ambiguity reviews.

## C1.2 The Dangling Else

The *dangling else* is one of the most common problems associated with requirements specifications. For example, the following requirement is incomplete (ambiguous), since the else condition is never defined:

"If the user enters a alpha-numeric string that is greater than two characters and less than eighty, a second prompt is provided."

The question now is whether or not an error condition occurs as a result of the user not satisfying the requirements of the first statement. Is this a fatal or recoverable condition? The dangling else is one of the most common mistakes in the definition of functional requirements and, therefore, product source code.

## C1.3 Reference Ambiguity

Another common problem associated with many functional specifications is reference ambiguity. This problem occurs when there are terms, acronyms, or other words which result in ambiguity of use. For example:

"Enter a number at the first prompt and add it to a counter."

One problem with the preceding statement is that there are several "counters." Therefore, the reference to the term, "counter" is ambiguous. The term, "first prompt" is another example of reference ambiguity. After all, there are potentially many windows which have a "first prompt" displayed.

## C1.4 Scope of Action Ambiguity

Scope of action is an even more complicated problem which occurs when there are many potential application state transitions. For example, a compound statement with multiple predicates, such as:

"If the user is experience level 2, or has root access, then accept the amount provided as input, update the database and print the accepted message. Otherwise, if the experience level is 1, then print the message 1."

There are obviously many dangling else conditions. Also, there are potentially many messages that are not relevant to the current context. Make sure to review the scope of action for each potential combination of scenarios using a truth table (i.e., create an extended finite state machine—a state machine with history).

## C1.5 Ambiguities of Omission

Errors or ambiguities of omission are another common problem with functional specifications or other documents. Omission ambiguities occur when a cause is provided without a corresponding effect. In other words, an input is provided, but a specific output is not defined or established. This greatly reduces the product testability and reachability during functional testing. Alternatively, effects without causes are also problematic. This occurs when an output is established without a corresponding input. Other ambiguity omissions include simply missing the cause or effect altogether (i.e., input, output, or both).

The following example depicts a cause without an effect:

"Out of space and permission conditions produce this message. It is also possible ownership conditions."

The next example shows the difficulties associated with having effects without causes:

"A warning message is sometimes provided. The user may need to use the **sync** command multiple times."

Missing causes are a common error of omission. For example:

"If you enter a valid command, it is executed." (This assumes that you have access to the command and that you have permission to execute it.)

Missing effects are a common source for requirements error. For example:

"If you enter an invalid command, the command is not executed." This does not fully describe the outcome which will occur. An error message is also potentially provided by the system.

Complete omissions are also problematic and commonly found in many functional specifications. This error occurs when the customer is not solicited for input regarding a new product or feature. As a result, the use-model is incomplete, or lacks key capabilities required by the customer.

## C1.6  Logical Operator Ambiguity

Logical operators are another very common source of confusion and ambiguity. For example, the following statement is not clear; is the condition based upon an exclusive or inclusive "or":

"If the user is the superuser or is on a trusted host, then the user may read the file." (Does this mean that the user is always logged in as root to read the file?)

The alternative is when the user is logged into a system which provides access to the file (i.e., a trusted host). This is a common problem with the use of an inclusive vs. exclusive "or."

The logical "and" operator is also sometimes problematic. For example:

"If there is disk space available and the user has write permission, a file creation or modification is possible."

One problem with the logical "and" operator is that it may contain many different contexts. For example, the condition (the user can write or modify a file) is only true if and only if both conditions are present. Alternatively, the write or modify condition is true if the sum of both conditions are present. For example:

"A and B produce C."

The "not or," "neither or," and "nor" conditions can get really tricky. For example:

"If not X or Y, then Z."

"If neither X nor Y, then Z."

"If neither X or Y, then Z."

"If not X and not Y, then Z."

"If X or Y are both missing, then Z."

"Valid inputs are X and Y. If none of the above produce Z."

The double negative is always more difficult for the human mind to grasp than the positive form. Always avoid the "neither nor" types of expressions. It is especially important to consider proper precedence when using special operators. For example, the following two examples are quite different depending on where the parenthesis are used:

"If not (X and Y) then Z." This could mean one of many possibilities:

1.  If it is not X and Y together then Z.
2.  As long as X and Y are not together then Z.
3.  Produce Z unless Z and Y are both present.
4.  If it is not X or it is not Y then produce Z.

Implicit connectors are another area for confusion and ambiguity. This occurs when multiple statements are joined together. The net result is a contradiction or ambiguity. For example:

"If either Bill or Fred, Nancy will go to the dance."

"If Bill does not go with Mary, Nancy will go to the dance."

"If Fred does not go with Mildred, Nancy will go to the dance."

It is extremely important to define and use an operator between statements, as this will clarify the relationship between each event. For example:

"If either Bill or Fred go

and

"If Bill does not go with Mary

and

"If Fred does not go with Mildred,

then Nancy will go to the dance."

Compound logical operators can be very confusing and provide significant ambiguity. It is critical to use parenthesis to "chunk" or group items together around each operator. For example:

"If X or Y and Z then print Hello World." This is poor.

"If (X or Y) and Z then print Hello World." This is better.

## C1.7 Negation Ambiguity

It is important to avoid not and nor expressions in functional specifications and requirements documents. As humans, we think in terms of "what is" much better than "what is not." For example:

"If my teeth are neither not brushed nor I miss my next cleaning appointment, I will receive a good report from the dentist."

Instead make it straightforward and avoid unnecessary negation:

"If my teeth are brushed and I make my next cleaning appointment, I will receive a good report from the dentist."

Notice also that we have avoided the double negative of "neither not." This makes the statement much easier to understand.

## C1.8  Ambiguous Statements

Many components in a functional specification can lead to ambiguity, for example, verbs, variables, aliases, adjectives, and adverbs. Some of many potential ambiguous verbs include:

- Compute
- Upgrade
- Change
- Determine

Good programming practice always attempts to use variable names that are mnemonic. In other words, we are able to easily determine the intended meaning from the name of the variable. The principle of variable ambiguity also applies to the terms which are used in describing functional requirements or a detail design, for example the variable names:

- InputField
- OutputAmount
- XYZ

The same principle applies to user-defined types, structures, functions, operators, etc.

Ambiguous adjectives are another potential source for ambiguity. It is useful to identify these types of problems during a functional requirements review. For example:

"The user must not allow the desktop to become cluttered."

"It is against the law to ride down the street on an ugly horse."

Law in Wilbur, Washington.

Ambiguous adverbs are also a common source of confusion. Just about everyone has seen a functional specification that includes one of the following problems:

"The user interface must be easy to use."

"The user interface must be easy to learn."

"The performance of the system must be fast."

## C1.9  Random Organization and Ambiguity

It is important to not mix functional inputs and outputs when describing a function or documenting an operation. For example:
"If X and Y then Z.
If A and B then C.
A will also result in Z."
The organization between the first two statements is muddled and therefore ambiguous. Make sure to use conjunctive operators to link statements for proper organization.

## C1.10  Ambiguities of Built-in Assumptions

This class of problems generally occur when assumptions about the reader's knowledge are assumed. Therefore, ambiguity arises because the context of the statement is unclear. For example, here is an instance of assumed functional knowledge:
"It is used as multiplier and then counter to determine the difference between the two data structure's members."
What is used as a multiplier? A counter for what? Which data structure and which members?

Assumed knowledge of environmental constraints is another critical check that results in ambiguous requirements, designs, and other workproducts. The relationship between the entities must be clearly defined (e.g., one-to-one, one-to-many, many-to-many, etc.). One primary aspect of testing is to determine if relationships are correct. Another is to determine if the precedence of the relationship is correct. In order to perform this task, the relationship must be clearly defined as to precedence, environment, and functional knowledge.

## C1.11  The "etc." Ambiguity

The term "etc." in a functional specification is a good indication that the writer has not had adequate time to complete the research necessary to fully understand the customer's requirements. A requirement document must be considered an agreement. In order for the requirements document to be useful, the agreement must be complete, correct, and unambiguous. Always be careful of delivering products whose development has been based on functional specifications which contain the term "etc.". In many cases, you may be writing a blank check for functionality, depending on the customer (i.e., the U.S. government). In other words, all the requirements either are or are not understood. If they are not understood, make sure both parties understand this fact. Try to avoid using the term "etc."

## C1.12 The "i.e." vs. "e.g." Cases of Ambiguity

The definition of "i.e." is "id est", or "that is." This case is used to explicitly define the members of a set and should never be incomplete. In other words, you must not use the term "etc." after the term "i.e." has been used. The definition of "e.g.," "exempli gratia," or "for example," provides a sample set which is either complete or incomplete. If the set of terms is incomplete, the term "etc." is tagged on the end. (See the warning in the preceding section.) Make sure not to confuse the terms "i.e." with "e.g." and vice versa.

## C1.13 Temporal Ambiguity

Temporal ambiguity is another problematic area for functional specifications. This ambiguity occurs frequently with transaction processing systems, where events must occur within specific time quantum. The following example shows the potential danger of time ambiguity, since the time element is undefined:

"The deposit to the account will be posted to the general ledger system."

"All local integrations will be promoted to central integration."

## C1.14 Boundary Ambiguity

Boundary ambiguity is common in many functional requirements and detail design specifications. This problem occurs when vertex or extreme points are not specified as part of domain testing analysis. For example:

"When the integer value is positive and the user's name is not root a special prompt will be provided, otherwise a warning message will be provided." (Is the integer value 0 considered positive?)

"When your adjusted gross income is $90,000 or less you will be in the 28 percent tax bracket, when it is $140,000 or less you will be in the 31 percent tax bracket." (What happens if you make more than $140,000?)[*]

---

[*] We all know the answer to this question—the government just takes more.

# Verification
# and Validation Best
# Practices Survey

## D1.1  Introduction to a Best Practices Survey

The following survey has been used to determine best practices and areas which require improvement for verification and validation. The audience for the following survey is comprised of engineers, developers, testers, QA engineers, technical writers, trainers, managers, and other members of the technical staff. Use the following questions to develop and strengthen best practices. After the questions, common results from this survey are discussed to help provide a feel for the typical areas requiring improvement in most software organizations.

1.  Are test procedures approved prior to the start of testing? If so, how and who approves them?

2.  Are the test hardware and software acceptable and controlled?

3.  Are all tests conducted in compliance with a test procedure?

4.  Are all software and test deficiencies discovered during testing recorded?

5.  Are all test data recorded and do they reflect the actual findings of the test?

6.  Are all software corrections retested? If so, by whom?

7.  Is all test documentation maintained to allow repeatability of tests?

8.  Are test status reports accurately maintained?

9. Do test reports reflect the requirements of the test?

10. Is design documentation updated to reflect changes made during testing? (This is seldom performed; however, it is very important.)

11. Is there a time when testing is complete, problems are resolved, and software is acceptable for the next phase of testing or for delivery?

12. What is the testing philosophy and methodology employed and are alternate test methods considered for achieving acceptance of the software?

13. Who are the personnel required to support the test program, including the number of people and their qualifications in terms of training, organizational affiliation, and experience?

14. What computer facilities are required to conduct testing?

15. Is any test software required to support the test programs?

16. Do test schedules, including locations, test configurations, and test-flow diagrams apply?

17. Is there a correlation between all software and design requirements to individual tests? (This question is a critical!)

18. Is the plan based on performance, interface, and test requirements?

19. Is there a test plan for checkout of each software module written, as well as a test plan to verify that the system meets the requirements?

20. Is there a description of all tests to be performed, including inputs, test conduct, and expected results? (The expected results must include the measurement tolerances and acceptance criteria.)

21. Are test results obtained in each test?

22. Does the test plan encompass an integrated test cycle from the system level down to the lowest level?

23. Does each test verify at least one requirement and is each requirement verified in a test?

24. Are all tests accomplished with the test software and equipment identified?

**25.** Are the tests performed in a logical sequence, so that early test results can be used in later tests?

**26.** Do the tests verify interface compatibility?

**27.** Are there no areas of over-testing or under-testing? (This is one of my favorites.)

**28.** Are all supporting resources identified? Does this include beta sites and third parties that will help in the validation process?

**29.** Are the responsibilities of the test participants identified?

**30.** Is the description of each test sufficient for correct test conduct?

**31.** Does marketing provide a good feeling for which features are important to the customers and how the product is positioned in the marketplace? (This is another critical question.)

**32.** Are the criteria for success or failure of each test unambiguously clear?

**33.** Are the test inputs and outputs identified and listed?

**34.** Is sufficient consideration given to data storage and data reduction?

**35.** Is the test schedule compatible with the design cycle?

**36.** Are the actual results of each test listed and compared with the predicted results?

**37.** Do the test results meet the acceptance criteria?

**38.** If the software under test were responsible for a device that activated a rip cord on a parachute, would you test it more?

**39.** What three attributes best describe the product assurance group?

**40.** What three attributes best describe the engineering group?

**41.** How would you best describe the current relationship between the product assurance (QA) and the engineering groups? Why is it a success or failure?

**42.** What else do you feel is important and relevant about the current situation? What tools, processes, and technology are lacking?

**43.** Please rate the following software quality product factors from 1 (low) to 5 (high):
  **a.** Correctness
  **b.** Efficiency
  **c.** Flexibility
  **d.** Integrity
  **e.** Interoperability
  **f.** Maintainability
  **g.** Portability
  **h.** Reliability
  **i.** Reusability
  **j.** Testability
  **k.** Usability

**44.** Please rate the following people-ware (project team member) quality factors from 1 (low) to 5 (high):
  **a.** Correctness (cross-functional and intact team environments)
  **b.** Efficiency (gets things done)
  **c.** Flexibility (ability to adapt to change)
  **d.** Integrity (yes means yes; no means no)
  **e.** Interoperability (communication skills)
  **f.** Maintainability (fit, good health, spirit, etc.)
  **g.** Portability (versatile, multi-functional)
  **h.** Reliability
  **i.** Reusability (memory, efficient)
  **j.** Testability (can locate and isolate problems)
  **k.** Usability (can get the job done easily)

## D1.2  Typical Results from The Preceding Survey

The following statements and comments may seem somewhat negative; however, they are quite typical of most software development organizations. Do not be alarmed at the number of problem areas, as software development and engineering is a fairly new engineering discipline compared with others (e.g., structural, mechanical). Try to find suggestions that are applicable to your organization and then prioritize the list.

### Test Plans

- All products are usually under-tested, few areas are over-tested.
- Test plans and QA plans are usually only created by the quality function.
- Most all test plans could be improved (e.g., more comprehensive).

- The execution order of most tests is often not considered in the plan. This can result in a single failure propagating throughout the entire test execution run.
- Engineering often does not create a formal test plan during the development process.
- You must know the product technology very well in order to write a successful test plan.

### Planning and Estimation

- All too often, too many releases are built to successfully test each release (code churn).
- Engineering always under-estimates the amount of time required to complete all tasks in the project schedule (e.g., unit test design, development, and execution are often not even considered).
- Application engineers are often not included in the plan and are key members who are required to successfully perform expert user testing.
- R&D hardware resources are often insufficient for successful integration and system testing.
- Communication is often difficult due to international and cross-functional teams.
- Too many releases, and lack of time and people often result in poor-quality products. (Planning and estimation is key!)

### Function and Unit Test

- QA must help R&D perform unit testing, therefore, insufficient time is available for customer use-model and acceptance testing.
- There is often no sharing of tests between R&D, QA, and customers, because a standard test harness is not used.
- Interface compatibility is often only tested at the GUI layer, not API.
- Test documentation is often poor if it exists at all (e.g., README files).
- There is often political pressure to "make the tests pass." Therefore, the meaning of reaching a project milestone is often diluted.
- Engineers are often trapped in an algorithm and implementation world and are often not allowed to visit customers.

## Concept Proposal, Functional and Design Specifications

- Customer requirements data is often lacking and is not incorporated into the project schedule.
- The marketing concept proposal document is often only a template and is frequently ignored by R&D developers and managers.
- Tests are often not matched to functional requirements (e.g., functional test coverage).
- There is often no time available for requirements and design specifications (e.g., ambiguous, inconsistent, incomplete).
- Design documents are often not updated during the unit, integration, and test phases (only user documentation is maintained).

## System Test

- There never seems to be enough configuration testing (e.g., peripherals, operating system and compiler versions, networking and other platform-related variables).
- The majority of the test process is ad hoc. Some (if not many) products only achieve a 0 percent structural test coverage score (i.e., are never executed and tested).
- Performance is often not very well measured (may require the assistance of a tools group).
- Some engineers often run nightly regression tests after a local change is made to the source code.
- Many companies never perform any type of multiuser or network testing.

## Test Technology

- More and better tools are usually always needed (support is often lacking in terms of resources). Use commercial, rather than home-grown tools.
- Complexity metrics are often not considered very useful (it is suggested that high-risk functions and source code be targeted first using risk and impact analysis techniques). Metrics include, for example, customer satisfaction surveys, defect density, complexity, and change history.
- Integration and regression tests are often used to conduct testing. It is important that integration tests actually focus on testing interfaces, and not stand-alone functions.

## Suggestions and Recommendations

- Unit, integration, and many system function and regression tests must be successfully completed prior to the alpha milestone (code and functionality freeze).
- Most companies need to drastically improve the tools and methods which are used for schedule estimation (e.g., CodePlan).

- Product requirements must be reviewed by customers (functional specification, design specification, architecture plans, and test plans).
- One major functional release per year is usually enough for most small- to medium-size companies. This release should be followed by an update release six months later.
- Longer and "real" beta periods are usually always required.
- An isolated test network using machines which have been freshly installed is very useful for single and multiuser testing.
- Test data files must be optimized and placed under configuration management control.
- Audit reports from QA must be optimized. Use filters for tools such as purify, **lint**, and others to reduce the amount of information overload.
- Customer use-models and flows are almost always never documented. Make sure to capitalize on this information and include this material whenever possible in user documentation and tutorials.

### Summary

Focus on three key areas:
- Test plans (engineering and QA)
- Assertion-based tests (engineering)
- Customer flows, fitness-for-use, and acceptance tests (QA)

# Root Cause Analysis Best Practices

## E1.1 Introduction to Root Cause Analysis

Root Cause Analysis (RCA) is a Total Quality Management (TQM) tool for process improvement. Unfortunately, this valuable technique is often ignored in the development and maintenance of most software products. RCA improves planning, as well as actual product development, by identifying the underlying cause of a problem. This process is performed using fishbone, barrier, change, or other analysis techniques.

Successful project teams perform causal analysis across the entire development life cycle (e.g., requirements, design and code review failures). Causal analysis is especially important for managing complex and difficult projects.

RCA improves both defect prevention and detection processes (i.e., verification and validation). In other words, RCA ensures that the right product is built right.

RCA is performed throughout the entire development life cycle, not just at the end of the process, or during a post-release review. The purpose of RCA is to improve the software development process using a continuous quality improvement model.

## E1.2 Benefits and ROI of RCA

Some of many potential benefits include:

• Not making the same mistake again (regressions and rework). (Most critical problems can cost thousands of dollars in just accounting costs.)

- Providing data to determine what development process phase needs the most improvement (phase attribution). Once the area of greatest risk is properly identified, the appropriate process, methodology, and technology changes are implemented.
- Providing more complete and comprehensive data that is available for analysis after a process change is implemented (e.g., code reviews really do result in fewer code-related failures and less faults).

There are many possible techniques for conducting root cause analysis. In fact, many organizations now conduct a post-mortem review at the end of each project to determine what did and did not work well. The following list includes some of the many potential methods for root cause analysis:

- Process of elimination (what functions the product performs, how the product performs each function, does the product perform the function?)
- Fishbone (four-pronged approach that identifies all issues related to people, technology, metrics, and process-related failures).
- Tree diagrams (and/, or task and other data- and control-flow-related symbols are used to determine the cause of a failure).
- Decision and condition mapping (identify decisions and conditions related to a decision; start first with a task list and add events).
- Barrier analysis (identify missing barriers for both the problem target and source).
- Change analysis (cause-and-effect mapping of changes which have occurred). Start from a baseline and identify all relevant deltas.

## E1.3  Root Cause Analysis Categories

The following categories are used to classify a problem during the repair phase. Problem tracking and management of internal and external problems is critical to project and product success. Many commercial and public-domain problem management and tracking systems exist. For more information see *UNIX Test Tools and Benchmarks,* Prentice Hall, 1995. The following categories are recommended for incorporation with the problem tracking system and are used during problem repair:

- **[R] Requirements**. The result of incomplete, ambiguous, unclear, or missing product requirements. Does the product do what the specification says, but not what the customer wants?

- **[D] Design**. A defect in the design when compared to the requirements specification. An algorithm, data transaction, or transformation problem. Does the product not perform the function according to *how* it was designed?

- [C] **Code**. A programming fault in the source code. For example, an uninitialized variable or wrong operator is used during computation. Is this problem the result of either a semantic or syntax-related coding problem?

- [G] **Integration**. A failure in the build process (CM items missing or process failure). For example, wrong library, object file, compile-time option, or environment variable. Is this problem the result of a build problem?

- [I] **Interoperability**. An interface failure between products (architecture-level). For example, a design flow failure where two products are incompatible (e.g., database and spreadsheet). Would a flow test contain this problem?

- [U] **Usage**. The customer is unable to use the product due to incomplete or inaccurate documentation. If task analysis and usability testing were performed, could this type of problem be prevented in the future?

- [S] **System**. A platform-related failure. For example, a failure as a result of the operating system, compiler, networking software, system configuration, or peripheral. If the product were tested with a specific system could the problem have been detected and contained?

- [L] **Licensing and Packaging**. A problem related to product installation and license files. If this specific licensing or packaging configuration were tested, could this problem have been detected and contained?

# E1.4  Responsible Parties

Each R&D engineer uses the root cause analysis field whenever the problem management command is applied to an existing report submitted by a customer.

The root cause analysis field is modified after verification (using the appropriate command to close a problem report).

The owner or author of the product source code always uses the root cause analysis field before closing a problem report.

R&D and project management must allocate time for implementing key process improvements in the project schedule. This time includes root cause analysis as well as action plan implementation (e.g., design and code reviews, unit test design, regression test development and execution, and metrics collection).

The root cause analysis field is optional at first; however, all products must perform causal analysis for process improvement and customer satisfaction. The RCA field often moves to a mandatory status after a sufficient number of pilot programs are completed successfully.

## E1.5  Root Cause Analysis Approach

The same approach that is used for conducting a structured review is used for RCA. In other words, the focus is on the process, not the person. If a group RCA is performed, everyone must come prepared. Ideally, a moderator, facilitator, and product owner must be present. See the chapters on design and code reviews for further details (best practices) associated with workproduct review.

## E1.6  Challenges to RCA

Categorizing problem reports and using this data as an information base for RCA is very difficult, since a limited amount of information is often available in the problem report database. Furthermore, causal analysis often requires comprehensive knowledge of the concept proposal, functional specification, design specification, and all configuration management items (e.g., source code, libraries, and compilers). Therefore, root cause analysis often seems extremely subjective; however, the following simple questions help provide categories for further analysis:

1. Does the problem have to do with "what" the function or system does (i.e., requirements failure)?
2. Does the problem have to do with "how" the system or function performs its function (i.e., design failure)?
3. Does the function or system perform the function as implemented (i.e., code failure)?
4. Is the problem specific to a particular platform (i.e., system failure)?
5. Is the problem a result of a configuration management failure (i.e., integration failure)?
6. Is the problem a human failure (e.g., mind-to-hand transfer of information failure, miscommunication, or other human interaction)?

## E1.7  Potential Questions and Answers During RCA

Should all enhancement be considered design, requirements, or actual code defects? Ask the preceding questions and see if through the process of elimination you can determine the best category.

What about product performance issues? Where do they fit in? How about usability? Complete performance requirements always include functional requirements. The majority of performance-related problems are the result of poorly defined use-models (i.e., requirements and design documentation). Again, ask the preceding questions to find the best match.

What if the text of a problem report is poorly documented so that the true root cause is unidentifiable? Do you skip that problem report? What process can be put into place to support root-cause analysis here? Usually you need to simply skip these types of problems. However, you may append a clearer description of the problem as part of your research. Remember, much of the information contained in the problem management system is documented to help the end user.

How do you handle duplicate problem reports? All the same? Usually you will want to treat duplicates as the same problem. You may keep a reference count to determine the importance of a problem (user population).

Does an interoperability problem, in fact, typically point to a design, code, or requirement hole? Yes, interoperability is either a result of a functional or structural failure. Ask the *what*, *how*, and *does* questions.

Should all problem reports which come with a current status of "void" be considered in a product's problem report profile when judging root causes and performing analyses? Usually you will rank a void problem report as a lower priority (below live problem reports). It is suspected that many void problem reports can be linked to usability-related failures in many cases (i.e., training, documentation, poor task analysis).

## E1.8  Common Causes for Failure

- Missing and/or incorrect information
- Training (experience, confidence, and education)
- Human peripheral or mind failure, or both
- Infrastructure failure (process, method, and tool):
  - Missing functional specification, design specification or review
  - Alpha demos of functional requirements not conducted
  - Cross-functional synchronization (communication breakdown)

# A P P E N D I X    F

# Best-in-Breed Organizations

**T**wo primary areas are emphasized by best-in-breed organizations—training and teamwork. Training is a very important part of the company culture. Having a training-oriented culture must start from the top. For example, general managers are reviewed and measured, as are all other employees, by how many hours of training are completed each year. Executive staff training averages between 40 and 80 hours per year.

## F1.1   Team Players and Metrics

Team players are strongly encouraged. Employees that do not play well in a team environment are often "de-selected," or severed from the group (even the company). Lack of teamwork results in coaching and finally counseling in many cases (i.e., termination of employment).

Best-in-breed organizations provide consistent messages that metrics are a critical part of the company culture. Engineers and support personnel live by metrics goals and results, since measurements work and help everyone to contribute to the bottom line. Best-in-class organization culture places a strong belief in metrics. For example:

- People are involved (i.e., the purpose is known early on)
- Coaches take responsibility
- Teams collect data and review/analyze information
- Metrics presentations are rotated (everyone must participate)
- Results are presented to management
- Root cause analysis uses metrics data

Metrics are especially critical for measuring individual and team success, because even best-in-breed organizations often reduce their work force by half.

## F1.2  Quality Days and Focus Working Groups

Quality days and weeks are very much a part of the best-in-breed culture. This includes quality awards where the team members present their accomplishment (required in order to receive a cash bonus).

Focus Working Groups (FWG) form a new approach to support the "initiatives" team. FWGs include an executive sponsor and various project members. Another approach to process improvement that has recently started is a Process Improvement Request (PIR). The PIR is submitted to the initiatives team, then forwarded to the FWG for implementation and action. Best-in-breed teams are able to successfully deliver quality products according to the project schedule. These teams are often asked by their customer to increase the turnaround time for product delivery. Metrics and process improvement scores for general managers and executives are tied to bonus and compensation packages.

## F1.3  Tools and Technology

Best-in-class organizations often use Computer Aided Software Engineering (CASE) tools for software development. These tools often support the underlying development methodology. Once the software development technology is instituted, project planning is much more accurate. For example, a standard waterfall life-cycle model for project planning provides consistent results (i.e.,it indicates when the software requirements definition, preliminary design, detailed design, unit code and test, and system test phases will complete). This is especially critical for the implementation and maintenance phases of product development. Using development-environment tools based on a methodology is quite different from ad hoc manual methods. Ad hoc methods and tools provide inaccurate project planning, estimation, scheduling, and tracking (to say the least).

## F1.4  Handbooks

Best-in-breed teams often have a program manager's handbook. This book contains a composite of standards for continuous improvement. (Every team must have this type of document.)

Successful project teams have requirements and design reviews that follow the standard Fagan rules for inspections and reviews.

Best-in-class organizations often conduct a process assessment (1-2 weeks) after implementation. This means that the company collects all relevant data and stores it on-line for shared access. This information can be considered an electronic binder book.

## F1.5  Requirements and Development Process Flow

Best-in-breed organizations were not always the best. Only three years ago, most organizations had no requirements (only a couple of bullets on a presentation were used for guidelines). Schedules were also top-down. Best-in-class software development organizations use bottom-up scheduling estimates. Therefore, requirements are better defined and schedule estimates are more accurate. Successful teams continue to make several iterations during the development life-cycle between requirements and schedule (nothing is ever static in software development). Feature creep can often kill the schedule and plan, and therefore it is monitored closely.

The development process flow is as follows:

1. Five to six people create a straw man (proposal) and perform some prototypes for small projects.
2. A sponsor team and users at large (five to fifteen people) review and comment as a group, or through one-on-one teams.
3. One to three people incorporate all edits and modifications to the strawman (draft proposal document).
4. The group sends a sponsor team to start the work.
5. The team now starts the development work according to the plan.
6. The plan is maintained throughout the development process.
7. A post-mortem is conducted. All critical issues discovered from the post-mortem review are collected and action items are assigned.

## F1.6  Training

Again, training is an important part of any successful organization's culture. This includes OOD, software test, reviews, and metrics. Successful teams use software productivity tools, such as Cadre's Teamwork Design product, for product development.

Coding standards for syntax, header blocks, and comments are also important for training. Bug prone, or highly complex modules are often selected for redesign, or redevelopment.

## F1.7 Schedules

Best-in-class teams do not have a single monolithic schedule which becomes obsolete when complete. Instead, successful teams decompose the schedule to determine clearly defined project and product mapping responsibilities. This process provides clear ownership (five people per project is ideal). Task teams, or high-performance work teams, develop project schedules and product requirements documents. Successful teams are able to negotiate using a win-win approach, and never lose sight of the end objective—products which delight customers. The following items are often negotiated between project team members:

- Team orientation (training, reviews, post-reviews, product planning)
- Schedule (management relies on the team for bottom-up estimation)
- Requirements (a sponsor team is selected—a privilege)
- Quality (goals/metrics are not viewed as having to do your taxes, but as critical data for successful product release)

## F1.8 Configuration Management (CM)

Best-in-breed teams follow documented processes identified in their software engineering procedures and policies documentation. These documents follow the IEEE and SEI standard for CM. However, most of the company's culture is sprinkled into the document (a working and living road map for success).

Testing of the backup storage site material is performed on a yearly basis. How many companies today have a process for archiving of critical data?

All change control requests are performed using sign-off forms. This level of formality is often required by the U.S. government.

Configuration management items include not only software, but all supporting documentation (e.g., requirements, design, architecture, use-models, and test plans). In many cases, documentation is the only workproduct which is under configuration management control.

Best-in-breed organizations focus on infrastructure (i.e., methods and processes), not just technology.

# Verification and Validation Outline and Checklist

The following outline is provided as a sample plan to use for Verification and Validation (V&V) of applications, or system software. The V&V outline is used during the product development life cycle to determine completed items. Checklist information is vital to project tracking and control. A sample checklist is included after the V&V outline. Project planning and estimation is also improved when V&V data is collected. Specific V&V phase deliverables are also identified in the plan for project management.

A template is formed from this document to contain example, or boilerplate text. Using templates provides both positive and negative rewards. One negative remark commonly made about templates is that the user focuses so much on the format that the content suffers. Conversely, having a template helps new users to understand V&V methods and quickly get started in the creation of an acceptance plan. Templates provide a good foundation for agreement between members of the project team (i.e., marketing, engineering, quality, technical publications, and technical support).

## Introduction and Purpose

a. Objectives
b. Background
c. Scope

## Reference Documents and Test Items

**a.** Requirements (functional specifications)
**b.** Design specifications
**c.** User guides
**d.** Operations guides
**e.** Installation guides
**f.** Application notes
**g.** Known problems and solutions
**h.** Release notes
**i.** Problem change requests
**j.** Others

## Testing Activities and Approach (Tables Are Recommended)

**a**. Features to test and not to test (R&D and QA):
    **a1.** Unit testing
    **a2.** Function testing
    **a3**. Integration testing
    **a4.** Flow testing
    **a5**. Regression testing
    **a6**. Reliability testing
    **a7.** Performance testing
    **a8**. Installation testing
    **a9**. Security testing
**b.** Item pass/fail criteria (expected results for each test)
**c.** Suspension and resumption criteria (crashes, hangs, and memory files)
**d.** Test deliverables (test plans, reports, tools, and tests)
**e.** Testing tasks (skills and dependencies)
**f.** Environmental needs (hardware, software, network, and others)

## Standards, Practices, Conventions, and Metrics

**a.** Approach (techniques, tools, methods, completion criteria, defect density)
**b.** Pre-release and post-release quality metrics
**c.** Test design standards (functional and structural coverage, code guidelines, documentation, and driver integration)

## Problem reporting and corrective action

**a.** Technology (problem tracking system or others)
**b.** Methodology for problem reporting and resolution
**c.** Records collection, maintenance, and retention
**d.** Metrics gathering and reporting (tools and measures used)

## Code and Configuration Management (CM) Control

**a.** Technology (RCS, SCCS, or other)

**b.** Methodology for CM and source code control

**c.** Tests vs. source code changes

**d.** Configuration items (e.g., tests, test plans, libraries, documentation, source code files, requirements and design specifications, etc.)

## Supplier Control

**a.** Acceptance tests

**b.** Acceptance test procedure

**c.** Technology and tools for management of product development

## Responsibilities

**a.** Management

**b.** Design

**c.** Preparation

**d.** Execution

**e.** Witness

**f.** Reviews and audits

**g.** Resolution of issues

## Staffing and Training

**a.** Customer flows and use-model validation

**b.** Customer tools

**c.** Product/tool skills

## Schedule

**a.** Test milestones (unit, function, integration, system, and flow-test phases)

**b.** Testing phase complete and accepted (test requirements approved and accepted). *NOTE*: This does not assume a big-bang approach to integration where all sources are integrated and tested at the end of the project. Instead, a phased approach to integration and test is recommended.

**c.** Installation phase complete and accepted

**d.** Release phase complete (to manufacturing)

**e.** First Customer Shipment (FCS)

### Risks and Contingencies

**a.** High risks
**b.** How to compensate (time, people, resources, and quality)

### Approvals

**a.** Engineering: _____
**b.** Quality: _____
**c.** Marketing: _____
**d.** Customer Service: _____
**e.** Publications: _____
**f.** Training: _____

## G1.1 Verification and Validation Checklist

The following checklist is used to evaluate and define success metrics for verification and validation testing. Also included in the checklist are criteria for acceptance testing. You must consider many of the following tasks at the start of the project. Therefore, the following checklist evolves throughout the project.

### Testing Activities and Approach (Tables Recommended)

**a.** Unit and function testing
[ ] Each functional requirement has an associated test. This is a modest means of measuring functional test coverage. Use-models, control-flow, data-flow, transaction-flow, loop, state-machine, cause-and-effect mapping, and other functional test methods are suggested.
[ ] Test matrix (functions vs. dirty tests). This table describes the relationships between functional requirements (from the user documentation, or functional specification) and the test library. Include in the test matrix tests for the following conditions:
[ ] Boundary values. These tests include values for minimum, maximum, minimum minus 1, and maximum plus 1. The program should handle all boundary values properly. This technique is now replaced by domain testing (see below).
[ ] Equivalence classes (these tests often include both valid and invalid data sets). This method also incorporates the technique of boundary value analysis and testing.
[ ] Syntax tests (often used for testing batch commands). For example, providing missing, incorrect command-line arguments, or flags.
[ ] Cause and effect mapping (requirements inputs to outputs). This technique is used to develop logic diagrams for the requirements, design, or source code. Boolean operations are modeled which include operators such as, "and," "or," "nor," and "nand."

[ ] State machines (extended and finite state models). State machines are similar to control-flow graphs. Finite state machines are tables, or graphs which contain state transitions (e.g., a light switch is on then off, or off then on). Extended finite state machines reduce the number of state transitions, since history information is always propagated forward to the next state. For example, a paste operation in a word processor only occurs after a cut, or copy operation has occurred.

[ ] Control-flow graphs. This method starts by creating a graph of all nodes (functions) as defined by the requirements specification. Next, links (interconnections) and link-weights are assigned. The purpose of the control-flow graph is to model all the various events and ensure a test is provided for each node and link.

[ ] Domain tests. This functional test method is more rigorous than determining boundary values using boundary value analysis. One of the problems (limitations) of boundary value analysis is that technique does not take into account the intersection of extreme or vertex points [BEIZ95].

[ ] Loop testing (reflexive and irreflexive) [BEIZ95].

**b.** Integration and interface testing

[ ] Bottom-up method. This method is used for testing a unit, function, or subsystem when the entire system is not available for testing. This method requires the use of a test driver to substitute for missing top-level functionality. (Explain the driver used):_____

[ ] Top-down method. This method requires the use of a stub file to simulate the behavior of a missing function, subsystem, or system function. A collection of stub files is often called a simulation library. The simulation library is linked with the program under test to simulate the operation of a complete function, or system [WILS95]. (Explain the simulation libraries used):_____

[ ] Each functional interface has an associated test

[ ] Execution of acceptance tests (function input validation)

[ ] Execution of data validators (function output validation)

[ ] Simulation libraries packaged (test stubs used)

[ ] Flow testing (customer use-models validated using transaction flows)

**c.** System testing

[ ] Product examples and tutorials

[ ] Documentation examples

**d.** Regression testing and CM control

[ ] All critical customer problems have a test written and checked into the CM system

[ ] All unit tests under CM control

[ ] All integration tests under CM control

[ ] All system tests under CM control

[ ] All system acceptance tests under CM control

**e.** Reliability testing (regression test build and execution cycle is recorded)
[ ] MTBE (Mean Time Between Error)
[ ] MTBC (Mean Time Between Crash)
[ ] MTBH (Mean Time Between Hang)
[ ] MTBD (Mean Time Between core Dump)
[ ] Other:_____
[ ] Testability analysis (e.g., weak and strong mutation analysis)


**f.** Performance testing
The time required for completion of the full regression test suite is recorded and compared with the previous baseline.
System Time:_____ User Time:_____


**g.** Installation testing
[ ] The product is installed on a freshly installed system
(Identify under environmental needs section below)
[ ] System disconnected from network and uses only local libraries and
    licenses.
[ ] Installation tests (product/package level)
[ ] Configuration tests (platform/system level)


## Item Pass/Fail Criteria (Expected Results)

[ ] Each test must successfully complete build and execution operations with-
    out any loss of data or functionality within the required time limits


## Suspension and Resumption Criteria (Crashes, Hangs, etc.)

[ ] Core dumps
[ ] Crashes
[ ] Hangs
[ ] Loss of data
[ ] Other critical failures (list)_____
[ ] Resolution of any of these activities is provided to resume, or restart test-
    ing activities

### Test Deliverables (Test Plans, Reports, Tools, Tests, etc.)

[ ] Unit/function tests under the CM system with test results
  [ ] Capture/playback test scripts
[ ] Test plan

### Testing Tasks (Skills and Dependencies)

[ ] Training with test harness and management system
[ ] Training with bug management/tracking system
[ ] Training with CM system
[ ] Training with regression test system
[ ] Training with structural testing and analysis tools
[ ] Training with reliability and testability tools
[ ] Training in coding and testability standards/guidelines
[ ] Training in requirements, design and code reviews
[ ] Training with capture/playback tools

### Environmental Needs (Hardware, Software, Tools, Network, etc.)

[ ] Hardware systems (include peripherals)

_____
_____
_____

[ ] Software (operating system, compilers, etc.)

_____
_____
_____

[ ] Network configurations

_____
_____
_____

### Customer Acceptance Tests

[ ] All critical problems are under CM control and are included in the regression test system
[ ] All expert testing (e.g., customer support engineers) and beta tests are collected for integration with the system regression test suite

### Standards, Practices, and Metrics (Values are for Example Only)

[ ] Each unit test is associated with a functional requirement from the marketing requirements, functional specification, or design specification

[ ] Each unit test is measured for branch or decision coverage
[ ] 75 percent or greater decision coverage required during unit testing prior to integration test phase
[ ] No core dumps or memory leaks are accepted during unit testing
[ ] 85 percent call entry/exit coverage required during integration test prior to system test phase
[ ] 70 percent function call coverage required during system test phase prior to customer acceptance, or beta test phase

## Approach (Techniques, Tools, Methods, Completion Criteria — Defect Density)

[ ] Each functional test includes negative tests as well as positive tests
[ ] Value equal to the minimum accepted value (from functional and design specifications)
[ ] Value equal to the maximum accepted value (from functional and design specifications)
[ ] One less than the minimum accepted value (from functional and design specifications)
[ ] One greater than the maximum accepted value (from functional and design specifications)
[ ] Data values equal to the accepted data type (from functional and design specifications)
[ ] Data values not equal to the accepted data type (from functional and design specifications)

### Pre-release Quality Metrics

List each pre-release quality metric for the following:
[ ] Memory analysis (static and dynamic)
[ ] **lint** or static checker (coding guidelines, etc.)
[ ] Stress tools used (list)
[ ] Test coverage (**tcov**, MetaC, PureCov, ViSTA, etc.)
[ ] Call coverage
[ ] Block (statement) coverage
[ ] Branch (decision) coverage
[ ] Static structural complexity analysis)

### System Testing

[ ] Test coverage (call coverage w/ **tcov**)
[ ] Schedule containment metrics
[ ] Content containment metrics

## Acceptance Test Procedure

[ ] Each functional test is under the control of a central test environment and is used by members of other project teams

[ ] Capture/playback tools are used to execute acceptance tests

# Glossary

**Acceptance Test** Formal tests (often performed by a customer) to determine whether or not a system has satisfied predetermined acceptance criteria. These tests are often used to enable the customer (either internal or external) to determine whether or not to accept a system.

**Alpha Testing** Testing of a software product or system conducted at the developer's site by the customer [YOUN89].

**Automated Testing** Software testing which is assisted with software technology that does not require operator (tester) input, analysis, or evaluation.

**Baseline** A process where control is placed on all configuration items including sources, libraries, compilers, include files, test suites, test plans, and any other items required to build a product.

**Baseline File** A file that contains data used as a baseline for regression test comparisons (also known as back-to-back testing). This file is also commonly called a golden file.

**Bashers** Term often used for hardware-level diagnostics. The execution of many functional tests over the course of several hours or days.

**Beta Testing** Testing conducted at one or more customer sites by the end-user of a delivered software product or system [YOUN89].

**Benchmarks** Programs that provide performance comparisons for software, hardware, and systems.

**Black Box Testing** A testing method where the application under test is viewed as a black box and the internal behavior of the program is completely ignored. Testing occurs based upon the external specifications. Also known as behavioral testing, since only the external behaviors of the program are evaluated and analyzed.

**Bottom-up Testing** Test drivers are used to help perform unit testing with lower-level modules, even though the system, subsystem, or entire function may be incomplete.

**Boundary Value Analysis (BVA)** BVA is different from equivalence partitioning in that it focuses on "corner cases" or values that are usually out of range as defined by the specification. This means that if a function expects all values in the range of negative 100 to positive 1000, test inputs would include negative 101 and positive 1001. BVA attempts to derive the value just above or below the maximum and minimum expected value. BVA is often used as a technique for stress, load, or volume testing. This type of validation is usually performed after positive functional validation has completed (successfully) using requirements specifications and user documentation.

**C0 Coverage** The number of statements in a module that have been executed during testing, divided by the total number of statements contained in the program under test.

**C1 Coverage** The number of segments (branches or decisions) in a program that have been executed during testing, divided by the total number of segments in the program under test.

**Call Graph** A graphical representation of program caller-callee relationships. It is used to determine which function calls need further testing. Most useful during the system test phase.

**Call Pair** The connection between a caller and callee. Usually included in a call tree. See Call Graph.

**Cause-and-effect Graphing** A functional testing method that uses combinations of inputs that are compared with specifications for matching error conditions (effects).

**Complexity** A metric of the degree of internal complexity of a program usually expressed in terms of some algorithmic measure. For example, the number operators, operands, decisions, tokens, etc.

**Connected Digraph** A directed graph (a set of nodes interconnected with entry and exit nodes) where there is at least one entry node to every exit node.

**Cyclomatic Complexity** A metric of the degree of internal complexity of a program's flow of control based on the number and arrangement of decisions.

**Data Flow Analysis** Consists of graphical analysis of collection of (sequential) data definitions and reference patterns to determine constraints that can be placed on data values at various points of executing the source program [YOUN89].

**Data Flow Graph** A graphical presentation of a variable as used within a module or system. It can be expressed in either legal or illegal uses (transitions).

**Debugging** The act of attempting to determine the cause of the symptoms of malfunctions detected by testing or by frenzied user complaints [BEIZ90].

**Defect** The difference between the functional specification (including user documentation) and actual program text (source code and data). Often reported as a problem and stored in a defect-tracking and problem-management system.

**Defect Containment** The technologies and processes associated with discovering failures, defects, or spoilage before product shipment.

**Defect Detection** The technologies and processes associated with preventing defects during requirements, design, or implementation phases of the product life-cycle.

**Directed Graph (digraph)** A set of nodes interconnected with many potential entry and exit nodes. A program must always have one entry and exit node. Also known as a digraph.

**Driver** A software program to control either the construction and/or execution of tests, like that of a test harness. Alternatively, a device driver controls the use of a specific hardware device.

**Dynamic Metrics** To focus on the collection of metrics information for the source code while under test execution management or control.

**Equivalence Partitioning** An approach where classes of inputs are categorized for product or function validation. This usually does not include combinations of input, but rather a single state value based by class. For example, with a given function there may be several classes of input that may be used for positive or negative testing. If the function expects an integer and receives an integer as input, this would be considered a positive test assertion. On the other hand, if a character or any other input class other than an integer is provided, this would be considered a negative test assertion or condition.

**Error Guessing** Another common approach to black-box validation. Black-box testing is when everything else other than the source code may be used for testing. This is the most common approach to testing. Error guessing is when random inputs or conditions are used for testing. Random in this case includes a value either produced by a computerized random number generator, or an ad hoc value or test condition provided by the engineer.

**Errors** The amount by which a result is incorrect. Mistakes are usually a result of a human action. Human mistakes (errors) often result in faults contained in the source code, specification, documentation, or other product deliverable. Once a fault is encountered, the end result will be a program failure. The failure usually has some margin of error, either high, medium, or low.

**Essential Segment** One method of performing selective path coverage analysis. A structural testing method where the segment of a program (entry and exit branches) exists on only one path.

**Essential Paths** Another selective path method of performing structural testing analysis. Paths that include an edge which is not included in any other path (i.e., includes one essential edge) are identified.

**Evaluation** The process of examining a system or system component to determine the extent to which specified properties are present [YOUN89].

**Execution** The process of carrying out an instruction or the instructions of a computer program by a computer [IEEE94].

**Extended Differencing** EXDIFF is a component of the STW/Regression product from Software Research, Inc. This method of comparison ignores differences that are resident within a user-defined masked area. The masked area includes data to be ignored during golden file comparison.

**Extended Finite State Machines (EFSM)** An EFSM is a Finite State Machine (FSM) with an additional history-based context. The context often represents various aspects of the history of a session. Using variables and predicates as an example, subsequent events can be determined based upon their dependence on previous events (i.e., history). EFSMs often reduce the number of total states or transitions provided by regular FSMs.

**Exercisers** Test programs oriented toward the basic use of a hardware device, software function, or system feature. One example could be a tape exerciser that provides basic read, write, and compare operations using various blocking factors.

**Failure** The result or manifestation of a fault. When a specific segment of source code is executed under certain conditions, a fault may be encountered. This fault will result in a program or system failure.

**Fault** The result of a mistake caused by an incorrect step, process, or data definition. For example, a missing or extra code segment.

**Fault-Based Testing** Testing that employs a test data selection strategy designed to generate test data capable of demonstrating the absence of a set of pre-specified faults; typically, frequently occurring faults [YOUN89].

**Firm mutation** Testing is determined by some internal state that detects the mutant later on during execution (i.e., longer association or coupling).

**Formal Review** Formal reviews are technical reviews conducted with the customer including the types of reviews called for in DOD-STD-2167A (Preliminary Design Review, Critical Design Review, etc.).

**Functional Testing** Application of test data derived from the specified functional requirements without regard to the final program structure [ADRI82]. Also known as black-box testing.

**Harness** A tool or program to control and manage the execution of both micro - and macro-level tests.

**Inspection** A formal evaluation technique in which software requirements, design, or code are examined in detail by a person or group other than the author to detect faults, violations of development standards, and other problems [IEEE94]. A quality improvement process for written material that consists of two dominant components: product (document) improvement and process improvement (document production and inspection) [GILB93].

**Instrumentation** A process where source code is compiled or translated to an executable file that contains additional code for monitoring program execution.

**Integration** The process of combining software components or hardware components or both into an overall system.

**Integration Testing** Testing conducted after unit and feature testing. The intent is to expose faults in the interactions between software modules and functions. Either top-down or bottom-up approaches can be used. A bottom-up method is preferred, since it leads to earlier unit testing (step-level integration). This method is contrary to the big-bang approach where all source modules are combined and tested in one step. The big-bang approach to integration should be discouraged.

**Interface** The boundary between two software systems, products, components, or functions. An interface is usually defined on an information or data boundary. For example, communications to the hard disk device are usually provided through a set of interfaces defined in the standard C library (i.e., **open**, **close**, etc.).

**Interface Tests** Programs that provide test facilities for external interfaces and function calls. Simulation is often used to test external interfaces that currently may not be available for testing or are difficult to control. For example, hardware resources such as hard disks and memory may be difficult to control; however, exception handlers must be tested for proper interface testing. Therefore, simulation can provide the characteristics or behaviors for a specific function.

**Kiviat Chart** A graph that provides a method of viewing the impact of multiple metrics on a source code module or set of files. This presentation allows easy determination of values (test metrics) that fall either under or over the expected minimum or maximum limits.

**Makefile** A file containing a set of rules for the construction and execution of a program or test. Oftentimes it is used as the front end or back end of a test harness.

**Methods** Different from processes because they are closely related to the technical or detail aspects associated with accomplishing a task. Methods are usually performed by an engineer, rather than a manager.

**Mutant** When the existence of a data state error is discernible at a time later than when the mutant first occurred. A mutant can include either a valid or invalid equivalence class for program data or text.

**POSIX** Portable Operating System Interface for UNIX.

**Peer Reviews** Peer reviews involve a methodical examination of software workproducts by the producer's peers to identify defects and areas where changes are needed [PAUL93].

**Predicate** An expression contained in the source code that contains multiple groupings of program variables and/or constants. The following source code statement has two predicates. The first checks the value of the variable "a"; the second checks the value of the variable "b" if ((a == 1) && (b == 2)) {;}.

**Prototyping** Prototyping evaluates requirements or designs at the conceptualization phase, the requirement analysis phase, or the design phase by quickly building scaled-down components of the intended system to obtain rapid feedback of analysis and design decisions.

**Quality** The degree to which a program possesses a desired combination of attributes that enable it to perform its specified end use [YOUN89].

**Quality Assurance (QA)** Consists of planning, coordinating, and other strategic activities associated with measuring product quality against external requirements and specifications (process-related activities).

**Quality Control (QC)** Consists of monitoring, controlling, and other tactical activities associated with the measurement of product quality goals.

**Regression Testing** Testing conducted for the purpose of evaluating whether or not a change to the system (all CM items) has introduced a new failure. Regression testing is often accomplished through the construction, execution, and analysis of product and system tests.

**Reliability** The probability of failure-free operation for a specified period.

**Review** A review is a way to use the diversity and power of a group of people to point out needed improvements in a product or confirm those parts of a product in which improvement is either not desired or not needed [FREE90]. A review is a general workproduct evaluation technique that includes desk checking, walkthroughs, technical reviews, peer reviews, formal reviews, and inspections [STSC94].

**RISC** Reduced Instruction Set Computer, as opposed to Complex Instruction Set Computer (CISC). A CPU instruction set that is reduced to commonly used instructions for performance improvements.

**S0 coverage** The number of modules executed at least once during the system test phase.

**S1 coverage** The number of call pairs executed during system testing. For example, if a function requires no other functions (no call pairs), the S1 coverage will be 100 percent as soon as the function is called.

**Scaffold** A component of software that provides services to another component. Any software used during development to simulate the other component is called a scaffold. See [IEE91] for further definition of test driver.

**Segment** A branch that includes a decision-to-decision path within a program that is executed as a result of a conditional (predicate) expression.

**Soak Tests** Also known as reliability, or life tests. Often a set of unit tests that are conducted over the course of several days or weeks.

**St Coverage** Execution of all possible call pair subtrees at least once.

**Static Analysis** Looks at the complexity of source code. It has been demonstrated that highly complicated modules or functions are more error-prone and should be isolated for more rigorous inspection, verification, and validation.

**Static Structural Analysis** Can be provided without program execution and only requires a *map* of the source code structure. Includes McCabe's Cyclomatic and Essential Complexity, as well as Halstead's Software Science.

**Stress/Load/Volume Tests** Tests that provide a high degree of activity, either using boundary conditions as inputs or multiple copies of a program executing in parallel as examples.

**Strong Mutation Testing** A comparison of program outputs which decide if a test case was able to distinguish between a mutant and the original program state.

**Stub** A component that uses the services of another component. Any software used to simulate the other component during development is called a stub. See [IEE91] for further definition.

**Superuser or Root** The system administrator. The user that can access any file or directory regardless of permission settings.

**Syntax testing** A common form of testing where a command or function is often used (tested) without providing the required or necessary options or arguments.

**System** A collection of people, machines, and methods organized to accomplish a set of specified functions [IEEE94].

**Test** Any activity in which a program is executed under specified conditions, the results are observed or recorded, and an evaluation is made (test success or failure). A [unit] test is commonly used for testing a single module. Ideally, a unit test isolates test inputs and outputs to the smallest degree possible (only one input and one output if possible). A unit test may or may not include the effect of other modules which are invoked during testing.

**Test Assertion** A logical expression specifying a program state that must exist during testing.

**Test Case** A set of test inputs, execution conditions, and expected results developed for a particular objective.

**Test Harness** A test harness may also be called a test driver. It is commonly used to clean, build, and execute test cases, test assertions, or entire test suites. A test harness may include the use of a test scaffold. A test harness may also be considered part of the function of a test manager. A test harness is the same as a test driver.

**Testability** Analysis to determine the probability of faults hiding in the source code under test. Low testability often means that testing will be difficult, if not impossible. See the section on PiSCES from Reliability Software Technologies.

**Test Assertions and Cases** Test cases are similar to test assertions, however, a test assertion will test one specific behavior of a function. For example, does the UNIX **malloc** library call return ENOMEM when there is no more memory available for allocation? A test case, on the other hand, may use several behaviors (test assertions) in an integrated fashion for a specific purpose. For example, what happens when the **malloc** function fails while we are reading from a file?

**Testing** The execution of tests with the intent of proving that the system and application under test does or does not perform according to the requirements specification.

**Test Stub** A module that simulates the operations of a module during testing. The testing stub can replace the real module for testing purposes and is commonly used to test error conditions and exception handlers contained in the application under test.

**Test Suites** A test suite consists of multiple test cases (procedures and data) that are combined and often managed by a test harness.

**Top-Down Testing** Testing that starts with the main program. All subordinate units (features) are added to the testing process as they are completed; however, stub files can be created and used for units not yet complete.

**uid or UID** - Each user is assigned a unique **uid** after log-in to the UNIX operating system. This integer value is contained in the **passwd** file and forms the basis for file and directory access security for the operating system.

**Unit Testing** Testing performed to isolate and expose faults and failures as soon as the source code is available, regardless of the external interfaces that may be required. Oftentimes, the detailed design and requirements documents are used as a basis to compare how and what the unit is able to perform. White- and black-box testing methods are combined during unit testing.

**Validation** The process of evaluating the software under test against the functional requirements (preferably defined and reviewed by the customer).

**Verification** The process of determining if the products (outputs) of a previous development phase are acceptable as inputs. For example, product requirements must be complete (to an extent) prior to detail design and implementation (code development).

**Walkthrough** In the most usual form of the term, a walkthrough is a step-by-step simulation of the execution of a procedure, as when walking through code, line by line, with an imagined set of inputs. The term has been extended to the review of material that is not procedural, such as data descriptions, reference manuals, specifications, etc. [FREE90].

**Weak Mutation** When the internal program state immediately after the mutant is different from the state immediately after the original state (short association).

**White, Clear, or Glass-box Testing** Analysis of the source code structure (implementation) to determine the integrity, reliability, testability, and other related factors of the software under test. Test data are derived from the analysis of missing program control (e.g., executable statements) or data flow (e.g., missing variables). Approximately only 15 percent of all companies are believed to use any form of static or dynamic structural testing or analysis.

# References

ADRI82      Adrion, W.R., et al., "Validation, Verification, and Testing Computer Software," June 1982.

BEIZ84      Beizer, Boris (1984) *Software System Testing and Quality Assurance.* Van Nostrand Reinhold Company, Inc.

BEIZ90      Beizer, Boris. (1990) *Software Testing Techniques.* Van Nostrand Reinhold Company, Inc.

BEIZ95      Beizer, Boris (1995) *Black Box Testing.* John Wiley & Sons, Inc.

BOEH81      Boehm, B. (1981). *Software Engineering Economics,* Prentice-Hall, Inc.

BROO82      Brooks, Frederick P., Jr. (1982) *The Mythical Man-Month*, Addison-Wesley Publishing Company, Inc.

COVE89      Covey, Stephen R. (1989) *The 7 Habits of Highly Effective People.* Simon & Schuster, Inc. New York, New York 10020.

CROS79      Crosby, Philip B. (1979) *Quality Is Free, The Art of Making Quality Certain.* Penguin Books USA, Inc.

DEMA87      Demarco, Tom and Lister, Timothy. (1987) *Peopleware.* Dorset House Publishing Co., Inc.

FAGA86      Fagan, M.E. (1976) "Design and Code Inspections to Reduce Errors in Program Development." *IBM Systems Journal* 3.

FREE82        Freedman, Daniel P., and Weinberg, Gerald M. (1982) *Handbook of Walkthroughs, Inspections and Technical Reviews*. Scott Foreman and Company.

FREE90        Freedman, Daniel P., and Gerald M. Weinberg, *Handbook of Walkthroughs, Inspections, and Technical Reviews: Evaluating Programs, Projects, and Products,* Third Edition, Dorset House Publishing, Co., 1990.

GILB93        Gilb, Tom and Graham, Dorothy. (1993) *Software Inspection: An Effective Method for Software Project Management*. Addison-Wesley, Inc.

GRAD92        Grady, Robert B. (1992) *Practical Software Metrics for Project Management and Process Improvement*. Prentice-Hall, Inc.

HETZ88        Hetzel, Bill (1988) The Complete Guide to Software Testing, QED Information Sciences, Inc.

IEEE94        IEEE. (1994) *IEEE Software Engineering Standards Collection*, The Institute of Electrical and Electronics Engineers, Inc.

IEEE_SOFT-    Yourdon, Edward. (May 1995) "When Good Enough Software Is
WARE          Best." *IEEE Software*. IEEE Computer Society

IMPA96        IMPAQ Organization Improvement Systems, "Accountability-Based Improvement Systems".

ISO91         ISO9000. (1991) International Standards for Quality Management. ISBN 92-67-10165-x.

MYER79        Myers, Glenford J. (1979) *The Art of Testing Computer Software*. John Wiley & Sons, Inc.

PAUL93        Paulk, Mark C., Charles V. Weber, Suzanne M. Garcia, Mary Beth Chrissis, Marilyn Bush, "Key Practices of the Capability Maturity Model, Version 1.1," Software Engineering Institute, CMU/SEI-93-TR-25, February 1993.

PRES92        Pressman, Roger S. (1992) *Software Engineering,: A Practitioner's Approach*. McGraw-Hill, Inc.

RIFK95        Rifkin, Stan, and Deimel, Lionel. (May 1995) "Applying Program Comprehension Techniques to Improve Software Inspections." Software Testing Analysis & Review Conference 1995.

RUMB91        Rumbaugh, James, Blaha, Michael, Premerlani, William, Eddy
              Frederick, and Lorensen, William. (1991) *Object-Oriented Mod-
              eling and Design*. Prentice-Hall, Inc.

STSC93        Software Technology Support Center, "Software Test Technolo-
              gies Report," 1993, STSC Customer Service Office.

YOUN89        Youngblut, Christine, *SDS Software Testing and Evaluation: A
              Review of the State of the Art in Software Testing and Evaluation
              with Recommended R&D Tasks,* Institute for Defense Analysis,
              IDA Paper P-2132, February 1989.

WEIN90        Weinberg, Gerald M., and Freedman, D.P. (1990) *Handbook of
              Walkthroughs, Inspections and Technical Reviews*. New York:
              Dorset House.

WILS95        Wilson, Rodney C. (1995) *UNIX Test Tools and Benchmarks*.
              Prentice-Hall, Inc.

WILS_TAM95 Wilson, Rodney C. (1995) *UNIX Tamed*. Prentice-Hall, Inc.

VOAS92        Voas, Jeff. (1992) *Improving the Software Development Process
              Using Testability Research,* "Proceeding of the 3rd International
              Symposium on Software Reliability Engineering."

VOAS93        Voas, Jeff (1993) Software Testability Techniques Seminar. Reli-
              able Software Technologies Corporation.